The Map to Spectacular ~~~~
in Business and in Life

SELLING

from the

INSIDE

OUT

…and a Sense of Humor is Helpful…

Thomas M. Redmond, Jr.

Redmond Group, Inc.

Copyright © 2011, Thomas M. Redmond, Jr.

All rights reserved. No part of this book may be used or reproduced in any manner whatsoever without the written permission of the Publisher.

Printed in the United States of America.

For information address:

Redmond Group, Inc.
43 Frost Circle
Middletown, NJ 07748

Library of Congress Cataloging-in-Publication Data

Redmond Jr., Thomas M.

Selling from the Inside Out/Thomas M. Redmond, Jr.

Library of Congress Control Number: 2010942222

p. cm.

ISBN: 978-0-615-53365-0

10 9 8 7 6 5 4 3 2 1

To Joanne, Sarah, Carolyn and, of course, Hannah.

My deepest thanks for your love, your encouragement and for putting up with my jokes.

Call Reluctance® is a registered trademark of Behavioral Sciences Research Press, Inc., Dallas, Texas. Used with permission. ALL RIGHTS RESERVED.

SPQ*GOLD® is a registered trademark of Behavioral Sciences Research Press, Inc., Dallas, Texas. Used with permission. ALL RIGHTS RESERVED.

The Fear-Free Prospecting & Self-Promotion Workshop® is a registered trademark of Behavioral Sciences Research Press, Inc., Dallas, Texas. Used with permission. ALL RIGHTS RESERVED.

Acknowledgements

I wish to acknowledge and thank those of you directly involved in the publication of this work. First of all, to my parents, Tom and Betty Redmond, for providing the gateway to a really good education and for making sure that the family never missed a meal! To Bob Swain of Swain Consulting for your consistent encouragement, "There's a book in there!" To Mark Hilton for your exceptional interviewing skills, your ability to manage my calendar, and your invaluable contributions throughout the text—it could not have been done without you. To Bob Middlemiss for your superb editing skills and particularly pointing out where different terms were used for the same thing—and I want to especially thank you for your enormously encouraging comment, "Wish I had the ideas presented in your book when I was selling full time!"

To Pablo Mandel of Circular Studio for your listening skills, attentiveness to detail and creativity while designing the cover, choosing the colors and the layout. To the others on the team, like Eric for production; Jennifer our typesetter; the production folks at Ingram Book Group; John Wopat for your help on the (happily) small legal matters; Sylvan and Dalit Goldwert of Merrill Lynch for helping to keep us solvent during the financial crisis; Geriann Smith of Valley National Bank for your encouragement and for renewing our company lines of credit.

To my business colleagues, who over the decades helped me and offered opportunities that were over my head. An enormous thank you to our clients for actually taking the leap and implementing these ideas and for continuing to teach me—thank you for your business and the confidence you have in our work. Lastly, thank you my friends and guides from around the globe. Somehow I landed in your lives, and my life became an astonishment (and that's a good thing).

Contents

Foreword

Miraculous visions, unfiltered peeks into the secrets of the universe, are granted to lucky people in some of the most unlikely places. My first such experience was on a New York to Seattle flight in 1995. I think it was over Ohio.

The difficulty with mid-air breakthroughs is that it's hard for other people to visit the site of the miracle and feel that inspired energy. The locations of in-flight "Eureka!" moments are practically pilgrimage-proof. That's why this book needs to be written, to bring the vision to you and lay out the Sales Process Map that somehow flew in through the sealed cabin window at precisely the moment I was sitting there with a yellow pad on my tray table and a #2 pencil in my hand. The map came to me, and I followed it right out of my successful twenty-five-plus year career in the insurance brokerage business and into Redmond Group, Inc., Sales Consultants: 1996 sales: $0; employees: one (plus Kinko's).

I love sales. I love my family. I loved them back when I went out on my own, on my inspired leap into the void. My kids were not too young and had developed an inordinate dependence on regular meals and a roof over their heads. All of the really big expenses—increased maintenance costs related to cars and clothing and college—loomed way large in the way too near future: the following Tuesday! So I had to figure out how to leave the security of the big leagues, go off on my own, and turn my map into a business while continuing to provide for my family. The Sales Process Map had hit me hard: simple, repeatable steps, steps I believed would produce meaningful, predictable outcomes.

I looked around and noticed that I only had my own map to follow. It struck me that it would have to do two related and weighty jobs immediately:

- help others to become more valuable in all important nooks of their lives—family, work, friends, community—by helping them to increase sales; and

- help me to navigate the void.

As Warren Buffett puts it, I'd have to "eat my own cooking." No net.

Oh yeah; my wife would hopefully go along with the whole impulsive shebang, and all the anticipated mayhem it assuredly would introduce into her otherwise secure and mostly satisfactory life. More about her later.

Things happen when they're supposed to happen; or they happen when they feel like happening. When the Sales Process Map came to me, I was riding the perfect wave, fueled by age-old spiritual forces:

- anger
- resentment
- frustration with my current job
- awesome fear
- all combined with an absolute belief that I knew how to help salespeople become more valuable than they already were.

The program rests on one simple principle: success in sales can be significantly increased, even assured, by following a systematic process. The light that went on for me is such a process. It unfolded, mapped out and fully formed, at 30,000 feet. But it didn't come from nowhere. At the time I was a producer at a top-drawer, New York-based insurance brokerage firm with 10,000 plus employees. I'd been a successful executive in property and casualty lines for over twenty-five years, a sales manager and senior sales executive for a few of the shiniest and blue-chippiest 10,000-employee brokerage firms in Manhattan. I even come from an insurance brokerage pedigree: a grandfather, a couple of uncles, my father, and two brothers, all in the business.

I'm now looking back over the past decade from a perch where I can see a well-fed, college-educated, on-their-own group of no-longer children (and even a grandkid!). I see satisfied customers who keep giving me new work and eagerly help me to grow my client base. And there's "personal dream" fulfillment beyond my wildest expectations, including artistic pursuits that have led to collaborations with top musicians on my own recording projects. Oh yeah, and there's the relationship with my wife. More on that later.

Seem like unrelated stuff? Not at all. If you follow this map, you're going to have to work on personal goals alongside professional goals. Work as a whole person, not a fractional person. Success in business cannot be detached from the whole picture, the fully integrated life of which sales success forms one (important) part. Your sales success will come most naturally when seen as a source of energy for moving other emotionally rewarding facets of your life toward fruition. Your professional life and your life outside of business are part of one big mosaic. To separate them is to prevent them from energizing one another; that's not the program. There's still time to put this book back where you found it and get off!

The approach is not high falutin' theory. It's never far from the playing field. For me, that's where I've spent all my time. It's what I know best. It's what I enjoy. And it also happens to be where they hide the money! Stick to the basics, and when you lift your head, you'll be more valuable than you were before. Energy we derive from a focus on *personal and professional* goals will power us. This is a street-level, basic-drill way of approaching sales. The in-flight vision highlighted a notion that had been staring me in the face all along: sticking to the basics, powered by the right energy, is the shortest way to the success and emotional fulfillment that surrounds us all, all of the time.

Best wishes are flying your way.

Tom

The Premise:
Why The Hell Has This Book Been Published?

Become even more valuable than you already are. This is the theme, the underlying driver of this work.

Selling from the Inside Out is a book aimed at men and women involved directly in sales and to those responsible for sales management. It is a presentation of Tom Redmond's Sales Process Map. Tom is a leading sales consultant to the property and casualty insurance business. His Sales Process Map is applicable to sales in general, in or outside of the insurance industry.

The book lays out a proven "street-level" guide to sales success. It is a day-to-day "what to do" and "how to measure it" map. It was forged in the trenches, not from B-school or behavioral sciences perspectives. It does not veer from hitting numbers. The "life outside of work" earns a place because it helps to make a better salesperson.

Selling from the Inside Out has a unique combination of high-impact, distinctive traits:

- Sales managers are tired of catchphrase-based sales training and skill enhancement solutions. While proven underlying sales theories exist, the sales professional and sales manager are interested in the most practical direct path to the goal line.

- The Sales Process Map is not theory. It's a square-by-square linear routine that details the un-glamorous daily steps that will get the salesperson to the required production level.

- Mathematical modeling of simple and incredibly powerful sales tracking protocols.

- Course correction. Automatic leading indicators of those areas that need active and engaged adjustment in order to reach and exceed goals.

- Individual or company Sales Process breakdowns are uncovered and remedies are formulated, applied, and followed up on.

From the "inside out"—what does this mean? We typically all have some definition for this term. In this book, the readers will focus on sales success as determined by their internal drivers, their "inside." These drivers are also responsible for every one of their accomplishments, every other aim in their lives. This book is an example: the internal driver of your author is to make people more valuable than they already are. The internal driver of your author is that this book has to be published, it has to be accessed, and it has to be in the world.

How did this happen, and why the hell has this book been published?

Your author experienced a curious vision on a New York to Seattle business trip, somewhere over (probably) Ohio. The vision convinced him to abandon his long-term successful big company career and head off on his own. It outlined a Sales Process Map; he wrote it down on a yellow pad with a #2 pencil. His internal dialogue told him to follow the map and ignore his "buts" about family obligations and personal financial ruin. The vision receded, back through the cabin window from whence it (apparently) had come.

Your author was ready to take the leap.

He took it and realized that the only thing he had to hold on to (besides loved ones and passions) was the map itself. He held on to all of them, just in case. And they turned out (altogether) to be the necessary ingredients for success and fulfillment. He's sort of a "street-level" guy, not given to theorizing over much, and he has found that the map, in fact, produces results. Incredible results for him, all of those around him, and all of those who pay for his services.

OK, so it's impossible for you to make a pilgrimage to the site of the vision. It was at about 35,000 feet, give or take, and maybe over Michigan, not Ohio. Fortunately, this book is way more useful than a pilgrimage.

Selling from the Inside Out: The Map to Spectacular Sales Success in Business and in Life ...and a Sense of Humor is Helpful.... The top line is that if you follow this map, sales come in.

Best wishes are flying your way.

...Oh, and turn the page to see the map.

(Your Name), Inc. Sales Process

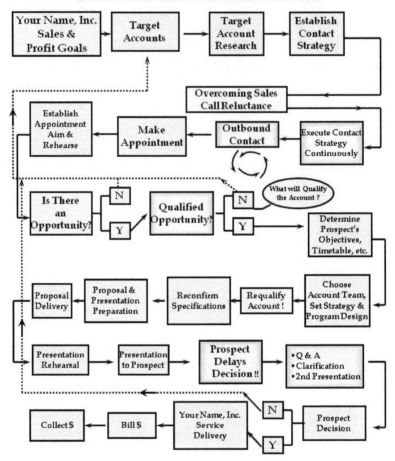

Copyright ©Redmond Group, Inc. 2011

Client Testimonials

Selling from the Inside Out: The Map to Spectacular Sales Success in Business and in Life... and a Sense of Humor is Helpful...

"Tom was literally the only sales consultant we *ever* let in the door! Glad we did it. Tom's programs had an immediate positive impact on our results. We wrote over $6,000,000 in new business in about the first ninety days! Through Tom's work, insights and ability to win over our people, we've changed our sales culture here at Hastings. This is required reading for anyone at any level in the industry who is seeking sustained personal and professional success."

—Bill Wallace, President & CEO,
Hastings Mutual Insurance Company

"Tom's approach to sales is "street level"—this is exactly what we needed at Kenesis. We're a great team of insurance, finance and economics professionals, but we are not salespeople. Tom provided us with a map to follow, critical leading indicator metrics, practical personal insights and customer dialogue skills that enabled us to develop and incorporate a sales culture into our everyday work."

—Jonathan Terrell, President,
Kenesis Corporate and Information Consulting

"Tom is brilliant and delivers what he promises."

—Stephen Schiffmann, President & CEO,
DEI Franchise Systems

"Tom's approach to Goal Setting has had the greatest impact on our team and me personally. The term "holistic" is really overused in today's world, but I must say that Tom's goal-setting approach incorporates both professional company goals plus personal goals. He is able to link the two as we've never quite seen before—to us that is "holistic" in the true sense of the word."

—Jay Fagan, Vice President of Sales, Acrisure Group

"Tom's programs had an immediate positive impact on one of our largest divisions. We were so impressed with the results of the pilot program that we extended Tom's work to over 250 of our sales and underwriting professionals."

—Dale Kelley, Senior Vice President and Division President,
Great American Insurance Company

"Who knew humor could be used to produce new business? Tom's approach continues to makes sense to us and is easy to follow. We particularly enjoyed his delivery and how we can turn our customers into an important part of our sales team. Professional sales people always need a good read, and this book is it."

—Allison Rhyne, Vice President, First Southeast Insurance

"Finally, a sales process map that anyone and everyone can follow; plus it guarantees an increase in sales. Tom's humorous approach to complex business issues is not only refreshing—it actually works! If you are looking for a fresh and novel approach in succeeding at your business, this book is it."

—Doug Witcher, CEO, Smart Choice Insurance Agents

"Tom has been a big part of our success here at Allied. Our sales team is more energized, focused and consistently productive. For years I've been after Tom to join our firm, but he's having too much fun working on his own!"

—Henry Lombardi, President, Allied North America

"The participants in Tom's program are consistently excited about what they walk away with and what can be applied immediately. Tom has captured the essence of successful selling and particularly what blocks salespeople from reaching their next level of success. He also delivers practical solutions."

—Wayne Nowland, President & CEO, Bradley & Parker, Inc.

"When Tom actually utilized his own approach at Redmond Group, new business flew in the door. I'm so glad that he actually has a job!"

—Mom Redmond

Chapter 1

GOAL SETTING
Let's Kick Some Butt

The Secret Is Unveiled

Mighty oaks from little acorns grow. Someone said that a long time ago, way back when verbs always came at the end of sentences. But we don't believe that all wisdom is ancient. It just seems that way. It can't be true that the storehouse of profound and wise guidance was used up in the past and that we're now left here clueless, walking into walls. Those old wise men and women apparently would like us to believe that they have a lock on all of life's major insights; the deadline's past, and there can be no further submissions. They've done a great job of promoting that notion. And we play right along with them. Ancient wisdom beats contemporary wisdom in any poll we've ever seen.

But enough of that nonsense! Ancients beware! The Sales Process Map rests on its own tiny acorn. And a mighty sales oak grows from it. Here's the acorn: The indisputable secret of success in sales rests upon *the number of contacts initiated with prospective buyers on a consistent basis*. That's it. The most successful sales people and the most successful sales operations follow a systematic approach to bring new business in the door. The Sales Process Map is going to show you how to channel energy (which you already have in abundance, and which can be increased) through a systematic series of steps that turn this simple statement into earnings.

We're going to start by thinking about, and directing ourselves toward:

- the number

- the number of contacts
- the number of contacts initiated
- the number of contacts initiated with prospective buyers
- and all on a consistent basis.

That's it, final gun; game over for the competition. We've relieved them of the burden of their business, generous souls that we are. Think of our work as a community service.

Now we have the key, the Sales Process Map supported by the procedures that will keep the indisputable secret of success in focus, and lead us relentlessly forward, day-in-day-out, to the Promised Land. And how can we determine on an ongoing basis when we've drifted off target? We build a special framework that supports us, that makes us *want* to stay at the center of our purpose.

Goal-Setting

Goal-setting is the basic material of the sales process map framework. It's also our compass, our radar, our course-corrector. We set goals with certain identifiable, essential characteristics. They're all musts. There are only a few of them. But they're all musts. They're foolproof. You can't help but succeed. We've assaulted them from all sides, and they've withstood all our mightiest attempts to flop. A life's framework built on the right kind of principles with goals properly handled has a special property. It moves us toward success. We can't stop it. We will set:

- Professional goals
- Personal goals

And these goals will be:

- Meaningful
- Measurable

- Written

Why are we doing this? To energize our pursuit of those contacts. To solidly ground our focus on the number of contacts initiated with prospective buyers on a consistent basis.

Secret #2, Unveiled (Two secrets so far. And you only paid for *one* book!)

The characteristics of the goals (above) and how we handle them—the way we write them, track them and evaluate our progress—are essential ingredients of a special brew. There's a *feel* aspect to goals and goal-setting that enlivens, empowers and strengthens the whole process. The *feel* comes from the mixture of the personal and the professional. It's simply not enough that you say to yourself, "I want to make a million bucks." There's a combination of goal attributes, and goal caring and feeding, that opens the door to an untapped energy reservoir which will fuel success. Yes, it's a renewable resource.

I can tell you that *this* approach works. I can tell you *how* it seems (to me) that it works. But I can't give you a "2+2=4" explanation. That's because it turns out that you receive more out of the process than you put in. You become more valuable than you already are. This defies explanation (at least from me). But I can bear witness to the fact that the sales process map has dramatically increased the sales of my customers, taken me to the top of my field, and enabled me to carve out a life that's more fulfilling and surprising than I ever thought possible. So let's take a closer look at the nature of this goal business.

Professional Goals

This is an obvious class of goals. After all, the reason you're reading this book is because you have been told to read it by someone who's responsible for increasing sales at your company; or perhaps you've stumbled upon it on your own and you think it might be worth checking out as an aid to increasing your productivity, making more money, advancing your career, starting your own company and making you more valuable than you already are. In any case, it is obvious that a book on boosting sales has, as an attribute, a focus on favorably impacting the sales profession and the people who march off to the sales front to make their living on a daily basis. Further on, there'll be an expansion on working specific, professional goals.

Personal Goals

This is perhaps not such an obvious goal category for a book about sales. But it's as much a "must" as professional goals. Looking back on my own career, I can see that I spent many years as a conscientious Company Man. I thought that the most honorable thing I could achieve was to die at my desk. No personal goals, just company goals. Here's how it might have played out:

Death of a Salesman II

A thud.

A few colleagues enter Tom's office. It's 9:23 PM, the Friday after Thanksgiving.

"What was that thud?"

"Tom's head. Hitting his desk. He's a goner."

"Poor Tom!"

"A heck of a guy! He worked his butt off."

"Dead at his desk. My, oh my. A real hero, a Company Man all the way."

"I'm sure he'd want his office cleared out so we can have somebody new at his desk first thing Monday. I'll arrange it."

"It's what Tom would have wanted."

"Can I have his Mont Blanc pen?"

"It's how he would have wanted it. Here."

"Thanks. Did he have a family?"

"Who knows? I'll send an e-mail notice to the entire department and mention you guys, so that everyone will know we were here this late on a quasi-holiday Friday..."

"Great!"

"...and to let them know that Tom died."

"Tom? Oh yeah! Him!"

Points at Tom and nods gravely, with furrowed brow.

The End

Here's an irony. Companies, and individuals within those companies, are best served in all regards—production, employee and customer satisfaction, and workplace harmony—when personal goals are in the picture right alongside professional goals, not down a notch—we mean right alongside your professional goals. Personal goals might include things we want to do for ourselves; activities that include family and friends, or maybe the community. They might (should!) include physical, spiritual and mental exercise.

These goals are important because they anchor our energy to pursuits that can give a huge positive jolt to everything we do. As we're pursuing our professional goals, we're simultaneously focusing energy on our personal interests. Our whole being is pulling in a concerted way, a way that hitches our feelings to the wagon. Everything we set as a goal, professional *and* personal, benefits from the fact that we bring our *whole* self to it. It's where 2+2 equals more than 4.

There are three characteristics in addition to the requirement that goals are both personal and professional. They must be:

Meaningful

The point here is simply to push you in the direction of devoting time and thought to the emotional stake that you have in the goals. The more important the goal is, on a gut level, the stronger and deeper the physical, intellectual and emotional connection is to that powerful energy reserve you're tapping into. Meaningfulness has nothing to do with the dramatic impact or magnitude of the goal. Walking your kid to the school bus five days a week could easily be more meaningful to you than climbing Mount Everest.

Measurable

Specificity in describing the goal is another requirement for ensuring high impact and results. Without going nuts, describe measurable features. A personal goal shouldn't read, for example, "Get in better shape." Write down a target weight, a target date, and a few words about the program you're going to start (e.g. diet, type of exercise, benchmarks...). The point, again, is to crystallize the idea by putting effort into the description, by driving toward specifics.

Written

There's no word-processing or typing or PDAs or other such old-fashioned keyboard digital nonsense in this program! We're strictly cutting edge here. Get a yellow pad and lead pencil, #2.

Seriously. The goals are to be written, by hand, on a yellow pad, with a #2 pencil.

It's not because I'm a magician that I insist on these particular tools. It's all part of deepening and strengthening the connections between our conscious intentions (the written goals) and the unconscious energy reservoir we're tapping.

Suffice it to say that the *way* we write the goals, including the materials we use, helps to give oomph to the whole undertaking. The deeper we go, the more outward manifestations we get. And writing by hand, with pencil and paper, takes us deeper into our goals. Trust me. No more questions.

OK, one additional point. Over the years, we've become convinced that writing is *the* way due to the fact that as humans we have been handwriting (and carving) for millennia—relatively speaking, we've only recently become typists. Have you ever realized that probably the most important class you have ever taken was high school typing? (But I digress!)

Lastly, the goals will be set for a few different intervals. Let's start with five personal and five professional goals (meaningful, measurable and written) with a thirty-day fulfillment period; three with a 90 day target; two, in each category, at one year; and one at two years, just for good luck.

There are a couple of "care and feeding of goals" topics to mention here. The first is follow-up. At the end of thirty days, you look at your list. Let's say that you accomplished three out of your five goals; what do you do? First, you write the word VICTORY next to the three that you did accomplish; this is a must-do. Savor your victories!

With the other two, reevaluate. Ask yourself if they are still meaningful goals. If not, then cancel or modify them and come up with a brand new five for your next thirty-day segment. If they are still meaningful, then move them over to your following thirty-day group and come up with three new ones. The point is not to beat yourself up about the missed two. Don't stop and stare. Drop, modify or carry them forward. And move on with enthusiasm.

Topic #2 in the care and feeding of goals is resistance. This is a critical component of the goal setting process. As we move along with goal setting, there will be exercises that require a little effort. Resistance will pop up like an annoying gremlin. This only happens one hundred percent of the time! It's a natural part of the goal setting process. Your internal resistance dialogue will sound like, "OK, here we go. Write things out. I knew this'd be work. Where am I going to find the time?" or "This isn't going anywhere, I think I'll lose this book, let's skip this chapter, what's wrong with this author and publisher anyway?"

As the resistors crop up, negotiate with them. It's negotiation with a light touch, something like, "Oh. Hello, Resistance. Welcome. How've you been? Just wait over there and I'll get right back to you." And you walk away purposefully forgetting to return. New resistors will appear. You do the same thing. Put them on eternal hold with a cheery, "I'll get right back to you!" Brace yourselves— we even recommend taking physical action, like walking over to a door, opening it and throwing the resistance out (with love). You can pick it up later.

Remember, we're sticking to the basics: practical steps to street-level success. That's where the game is really played on the Sales Process Map. And remember that our *whole* self is engaged: work, family, friends, interests and passions. The resistors don't stand a chance. They don't know what they're up against, and they don't need to know. Just don't give them a permanent seat.

Now as we move forward, here's a one-time-only free goal: Your first thirty-day goal, personal and professional, is to have your handwritten goals done one week from today. As you read this, did any resistance come up for you? If not, you're one of the rare lucky ones—if yes, resistance did arise, you're right on target. Now negotiate with the resistance and get on with writing your goals.

Here's an example of how a goal sheet might read, looking back from the end of thirty days. Of course, it will actually be on a yellow pad and written in #2 pencil:

Date: 10/26/10
Re: Personal and Professional Goals

30 Day Goals
Personal
1) Write personal goals within one week from today. VICTORY!

2) Research local yoga programs/centers: price, times, location, etc. VICTORY!

3) Investigate options for "get away" weekend with wife by end of month. (Move this forward to next month).

4) Have neck on guitar repaired by end of month. VICTORY!

5) Track down high school band mates from the "Neanderthals." VICTORY! (All except for our drummer, "Less than Zero," who hasn't been seen since the encore at our last gig forty-one years ago.)

Professional

1) Write professional goals within one week from today. VICTORY!

2) Re-read *Selling from the Inside Out* by next week's "Meet the Author" event at Barnes & Noble. Attend event. Obtain Tom Redmond's autograph. VICTORY!

3) Go through files and make list of all companies to which I made a proposal (within last two years) and did not get the order. Complete by three weeks from today. VICTORY!

4) Contact five of these prospects during the fourth week. Contacted three—move the remaining two to the second week of next month.

5) Get files off of my desk and put away within one month. [Drop this goal].

90 Day Goals
Personal

1) Enroll in yoga class.

2) Spend at least one evening every ten days in casual "out of the house" activity with daughter. Maybe sports, e.g. digging for clams, or an hour in the batting cage. Determine whether she agrees that proposed activities are enjoyable. Goal of at least 8 such outings within 90 days.

3) Join Weight Watchers next week, follow diet, be down at least 8 pounds at end of three months.

Professional

1) Read *PowerPoint for Dummies* and become proficient in presentations.

2) Buy fifty copies of *Selling from the Inside Out* and distribute to colleagues, customers, and potential customers. Encourage friends and in-laws to do the same. Within 60 days.

3) Re-contact ten customers that we haven't done business with in at least two years. Get appointments with at least seven.

One Year Goal
Personal

1) By the end of the year, write six new tunes "roughed out" for a new CD.

2) By the end of the year, schedule a trip to Europe for myself and my wife.

Professional

1) My W-2 earnings for this year will be $200,000.

2) By this time next year, I will have had two lunches (or breakfasts or dinners) with the president of the company and with each of the five department heads (e.g. Marketing, Administration, Finance, Information Systems, Legal, etc.).

Two Year Goal

Two years from today, I will be working on a CD of my own material, with contributions by top musicians, including Bob Dylan. (Hey, it's my goal!)

Goal Setting

	30 days	90 days	365+
Personal	5 ⎯⎯⎯⎯⎯	5 ⎯⎯⎯⎯⎯	5 ⎯⎯⎯⎯⎯
Professional	5 ⎯⎯⎯⎯⎯	5 ⎯⎯⎯⎯⎯	5 ⎯⎯⎯⎯⎯

Meaningful

Measurable

Written – *By hand*

Redmond Group, Inc., 43 West Front Street, Suite 17, Red Bank, NJ 07701 732-224-9444 www.Redmondgroupinc.com

TOOLS FOR GOAL ACHIEVEMENT

We've gotten the goals written and we've looked back, from thirty days, and marked our progress.

Tracking

Let's stop here and unpack one of the goals in our example, the goal that goes specifically to income. It's the One Year Professional Goal: "My W-2 earnings for this year will be $200,000." Under Professional Goals, we're sure that everyone has (or should have) an income level in mind. The area of income production has a special sub-program to enhance the probability of hitting or exceeding such goals: it's called *tracking*. It goes back to the key: the number of contacts initiated with prospective buyers on a consistent basis. How do we bring maximum focus and energy to the first part of the key, the "number of contacts"?

Tracking is a simple process to ensure that sales goals are handled with maximum efficiency. Tracking helps a salesperson stay focused on the key sales indicators and, in so doing, adds energy to the whole goal picture, personal and professional. Never forget that all of your goals, personal and professional, are pulling together to move you to success. They start working as soon as you write them down. Actually, they're working now, but that doesn't let you off the hook. Write them down; paper and pencil or bust!

Tracking enables you, at any given point during the year, to see where you stand. It's built on leading indicators that will show you whether a course correction is in order. If there's a gap between where you are and where you need to be to hit your goal, you'll easily know what to do. For example, increase the number of prospect meetings, go after larger sales, improve your hit ratio through better qualification of accounts, identify the best product, service and pricing mix in your target area—improving only one factor may be all you need to close the gap

Before we walk through tracking and the development of leading indicators, I have a confession to make. I had a lot of resistance to the notion of actually sitting down and figuring out what I had to *do* in order to *receive* what I wanted in the way of compensation or other achievements. My attitude was, "You go to work, you make a lot of contacts, and you see what happens," and "If you're tired and harried, then you must be working hard." This seems quite naïve now, but I was totally pinned down by resistors when it came to studying and applying some type of mathematical model or metrics to sales. And who likes to be tracked? Was there really a need to measure activities? And I was a good salesman; things worked out well for me. Could things work out better?

Let's face it—if income goals can be addressed systematically, the use of simple metrics could shine light on some of the great underlying activity requirements as critical navigational aids and course-correctors. Relevant metrics sharpen our focus and help us deepen the connection to our "whole life" energy reserve, as do the yellow pad and #2 pencil. They let us know early when we've veered off course, and tell us exactly what we have to do to get back on the beam. Metrics put the "what do I do next?" syndrome into the past. Each day, we can know exactly where to head in order to get where we want to go.

Fatigue and frenzy become signs of inefficiency and are no longer mighty banners of "hard" work. We can burn cleaner, converting a high percentage of our time and energy into achievement and all the enjoyment that success can bring to our family, friends, communities and selves. We can have more fun actually making money than puffing about how "hard" we're working. We can actually become more valuable than we already are.

What happened to my resistance to sales metrics? Well, one day I was sitting at my desk, and I asked myself, "How many new business appointments do I get per month?" So I went back over my calendar and figured out that, on average, I had sixteen new business face-to-face meetings per month. I'd been a salesman for over twenty years and I'd never thought to take ten minutes and look at my meeting numbers. I was stunned. Not so much by the sixteen meetings, as by the idea that I'd never taken the time to look at such a basic feature of my life in sales.

I went from that epiphany to sketching out the simple tracking system that follows. I backed into it when a simple question had struck me. I'd probably read dozens of articles about sales metrics over the years, but it happened when it happened. Search me. Of course, it could have been the sales training program I attended which went something like this: "Dial 9 to get out."

To illustrate the basics for achieving the income goal, we'll create a simple model. The numbers are arbitrary, just for illustrative purposes. Don't worry about the numbers at this point—just focus on the concepts. You can add or subtract a zero or two in these examples. The approach applies to any business; you'll just have to make some adjustments in order to tailor the example to the specifics of compensation in your particular field. The universal applicability of metrics and tracking results rests on the fact that it goes from an income target, backward to my old friend "number of meetings," and, in the process, reveals the key converters of numbers into earnings. (Ignore that resistor. Send it on an errand. Here comes another one!)

For illustration purposes, we're going to assume that the income goal of $200,000 is set by someone in a business where salespeople work on straight commissions on new business only, and that the commission rate is 20% of sales. So, in order to generate $200,000 in commission income, we obviously must produce $1,000,000 in sales.

> When it comes to compensation arrangements, the contracts are as varied as there are sales professional personalities. One or two common characteristics are about all we can find. It is our hope that these illustrations will make sense to our readers. Of particular importance are the use of the mathematical models and formulas available on our website as a free download.

Annual Sales Goal: $1,000,000

We want to land $1,000,000 in new, signed business. How do we get there? And how do we measure, on an ongoing basis, if we're anywhere near target?

Proposal Hit Ratio

We go back, over the last year (or for whatever period that we have adequate data), and figure out the dollar amount of our actual sales. We then figure out the total dollar amount of sales that we advanced from the proposal stage during that period. The proposal stage means that we've met the potential customer (probably a few times), that we've decided that the opportunity is worth going after, and the potential customer has decided that they want to take a serious look at what we're offering. We've made our presentations, answered questions, and gotten to the point of awaiting a yes or no on the purchase of our product.

Divide the dollar amount of closed sales by the dollar amount of proposed business, and you have a hit ratio. Let's say, over the year, we had $700,000 in sales, and we made proposals worth $2,800,000. That gives us:

$$700,000/2,800,000=25\%.$$

We land 25% of the business we propose. So, in order to land $1 million in new business annually, we must advance $4 million to the proposal stage. Divide that number by 12 in order to give us a monthly amount, about **$333,000**.

So, during any given month, we should have $333,000 worth of new business proposals in front of potential customers.

How many customers does it take to hit your numbers? That depends on the average value of each sale. Let's say our average value is $50,000 per sale. Therefore, to get the required $4,000,000 in proposals for new business, we must make,

$$4,000,000/50,000=80 \text{ proposals per year,}$$

Or, about 7 new proposals per month.

How many sales meetings does it take to generate one proposal? We look back over our calendar and figure, historically; it took 2.5 new customer meetings to generate one proposal.

$$2.5 \times 7=17.5 \text{ new business meetings per month.}$$

***In Process* new business required in the proposal stage at all times = $333,000**

***New Business* meetings per month=18**

These are your critical new business leading indicators.
Whew! That was easy.

Before we rest, how about a word about Leading and Lagging Indicators? OK then, we'll begin with Lagging Indicators. By definition, Lagging Indicators measure results at the end of a time period and typically characterize historical performance. Simple examples are Closed Sales, Hit Ratio, Total Customer Contacts over the last quarter, Total Incidents, Total Incurred Losses, etc.

The key advantages of Lagging Indicators are the ease with which they can be identified and captured. On the other hand, there are at least two challenges: these factors are always historical in nature and do not reflect current activities. Lagging Indicators lack predictive power in spite of the fact that we wish to believe that the opposite is true.

As for Leading Indicators, they measure the "drivers," or those factors that lead to the achievement of Lagging Indicators. Leading Indicators typically measure intermediate processes and activities. Examples include new business "in process" or in the proposal stage, appointment to proposal ratio, initial prospect contact, the number of new business appointments, etc.

Leading Indicators are predictive in nature and, when used effectively, will compel the individual and the organization to make course corrections. Every business has one or more Leading Indicators, and yet it may prove difficult to identify the best ones. An even greater challenge can be capturing the data. These indicators are often new types of measures with no history or regular usage within the organization.

So here's a rule of thumb—Set goals based on Lagging Indicators and set activities based on Leading Indicators.

Now, let us rest.

From a little bit of digging through our PDAs or calendars for some historical metrics, we've created invaluable leading indicators, guides for going forward and markers for evaluating our position. And we only have to set it up once. It's data mining at its best! From old Day-Timer to the bank in three easy steps. It's truly amazing that the information we need to set ourselves off on an entirely fresh track is sitting right in front of us all the time. And that the method for converting the information into achieving your goals is breathtakingly simple. By making the small amount of effort required to set up your tracking model built from your leading indicator metrics, you'll be taking a huge step in redirecting all of your energy.

Goals transport us; they'll whisk us along, silently and swiftly. Welcome aboard. We only use clean burning, super premium goals: a rich mixture of the personal and the professional. There's a special program that we apply to financial goals: it's about numbers. The number of contacts initiated with prospective buyers on a consistent basis—that's the key. Next stop: Targeting Prospects.

Your Homework:

Complete the Tracking Master one week from today—hey, that's a free goal.

Please refer to our website, www.Redmondgroupinc.com, for downloadable Goal Setting Worksheets and our Tracking Master. Also, why not sign up for our regular series of Webcasts and our free monthly Sales Coach Newsletter?

Chapter 2

TARGETING PROSPECTS
Weaving the Widest Net

Now we move from the first square on the Sales Process Map, Goal Setting, to the next square, Targeting Prospects.

Q. What are we bringing with us from Goal Setting?

A. Two things:

  1) the fuel that's going to power us through the rest of the Sales Process Map, the energy extracted from our inexhaustible reservoir: our written *personal* and professional goals,

  2) a tracking system that will show us, at any moment, where we are and what we have to do to course correct and hit the "numbers" component of our professional sales objectives,

  3) an incredibly rich and rewarding experience getting to know the author.

You might be saying to yourself, "But that's *three* things, not two." If so, then you've just earned your "Most Alert Reader" merit badge and have been automatically selected as a finalist in Redmond's annual "Now That You've Been Caught Paying Attention, Continue Paying Attention and I'll Guarantee That You Become Even More Valuable to Yourself and Others Than You Already Are" Sweepstakes. First Prize—To Be Determined. Second Prize —Undeterminable. Third Prize—Determined (but currently unavailable for distribution due to complications arising from international trade disputes).

If you didn't notice that the Answer promised two things but delivered three, that's OK. Now that you're paying attention, you won't miss the next opportunity to earn your "Most Alert Reader" merit badge. And you might still be entered as a finalist in the Sweepstakes, although no commitment as to the future availability of prizes can be made at this time.

We have before us meaningful, measurable and written (yellow pad, #2 pencil) personal and professional goals that provide us with a powerful energy source. We're keeping tabs on these goals against specific time frames, checking off completions and making adjustments when and where necessary. The key to the highway is, and will remain, the number of contacts initiated with prospective buyers on a consistent basis.

You've probably noticed by now that I'm not afraid to repeat myself. That's because I'm more a drill sergeant than a guru. My job is to make you more valuable than you already are and help you to relieve your competition of the burden of their business, not to help you capture bliss (stay tuned for the next book) or learn the motivational theory *du jour*. We're at street level. By the way, you might capture that bliss or become a motivational theorist as a by-product of the basics. That's OK with me. At ease!

A Boot Camp Dialog

Reader/Book Owner (by now you've hopefully paid for the book): I'm all fueled up and rarin' to go! Got my personal and professional goals written! So where to next, Sarge? Let me at 'em!

Sergeant Redmond: Glad to see you bought the book, and you might, by the way, want to pick up a couple of extra copies for friends. It's the Gift for All Seasons.

Reader/Book Owner: Yes, Sergeant!

Sergeant Redmond: So. Now you're prepped! All fueled up? Ready! Set!... Sit!

Reader/Book Owner: Sit?

Sergeant Redmond: That's right. We're going to the *Situa*-tion Room (sergeants are entitled to two horrifying puns per book) to do some cogitatin' and preparatatin'. And send that internal resistance off on a few dozen laps! Now!

Translation: We're not ready to head out the door chasing business just yet; we've got some situation analysis and prep work to do.

From Great Thoughts to Tiny Thoughts (We Can Do It!)

One of the best kept secrets in history is that it's tiny, well-executed thoughts that really change things. Why? Because small ideas are actionable, and small actions accumulate. Big ideas require so much energy and are so unwieldy that you might as well try and move a mountain in one piece as turn a big idea into a measurable outcome (and measurable is what we're after). Trying to execute ideas that are too big will turn you into an emotionally depleted, physically exhausted heap. You may need weeks to recover, and we want to spend our energy going forward, not on repairs.

A practical recommendation: when you have that big idea, that great thought, wait twenty-four hours and see whether it's still a brilliant idea tomorrow. You may want to make this recommendation to your boss as well. The result of this strategy is wise use of our energy, in bite-sized pieces, and arrival at the goal with a minimum amount of wasted straining and with power to spare. Again, we're on the sales side of the Professional Goals. We are targeting prospects.

Starting with "We"—what's the story? As a sales person, who are we? And who cares? Let's get rid of the "who cares" first. We're looking at the instrument that's going to be doing the identification, surveying, verification and ultimate selection of prospective buyers. Prospective buyers are part of the key proposition. (I suspect you haven't forgotten the key: Number of contacts initiated with...etc. Don't worry. It'll be repeated.) So we care about "we" because "we" is the instrument that's going to be doing the targeting. We want to get the most out of the instrument's capabilities and features. We want to be confident and comfortable in using the instrument. We want to know what the instrument can and can't do. That's why we care.

Specificity

A word before we begin to discuss the targeting instrument—us, the Sales Professional. Remember when we set up our goals in the last chapter? A point of emphasis was specificity. We don't write "Lose weight." We have a time frame, a goal weight, and an executable plan for getting there. We don't write "Record an album." We write down the number of tunes we want to have roughed out by a specific time. It's certainly OK to write down aggressive numbers for medium and long-term financial goals. But you're going to get there by quantifying the specific, individual, executable steps (number of calls, meetings, proposals, etc.) required to build to the outcome. That's why we set up the Tracking Master. Specificity applies to everything about the Sales Process Map, including Targeting Prospects. We aim to be as specific as possible when looking at ourselves and when evaluating targets.

Zeroing In

In analyzing the targeting instrument (us—the sales professional) and the prospective targets, we're going to start out by throwing the widest possible net in search of clues as to who we are and who might qualify as a target for us. We want to avoid leaving out any features of ourselves or of the targets that could provide a combination for success. Then we're going to sift through the catch and, using meaningful selection criteria, we'll end up with the most specific, identifiable characteristics of ourselves and the targets.

We're going to see where the evidence falls out most naturally, and then we'll probe a little deeper. We'll verify, aiming to line ourselves up with the richest, most accessible targets, the targets most suited to our instrument. We're not going to force a fit. That leads to wasted energy and disappointment. We want to end up with a natural bridge between our own distinguishing characteristics and selected characteristics of the targets. That's where the strongest, most rewarding bonds will be established.

This chapter covers two squares on the Sales Process Map. After we've gathered the best targets, then we move on to Target Research. We're not going to go outside of the situation room in this chapter. We're going to do some homework that will yield long-term benefits, helping us to get the most out of our resources.

You'll also find that an interesting characteristic comes into existence as an organic outgrowth of the steps we begin right here. Your permanent pool of prospective customers maintains a remarkably consistent size. In following the Sales Process Map over time, we've found that we reach a number of prospects (at Redmond Group and for many of our clients, the number is one hundred and six; I call it the "Rolling 106") that doesn't fluctuate very much. We win business and prospects out of the prospective account pool; or we decide that a prospect is not worthy of pursuing and take them out of the pool; or we get a referral, qualify/verify it, and add it to the pool. No matter what, it always adds up to about one hundred six active prospects. Don't ask me why it works out that way. It just does. So your homework is to identify one hundred and six prospects/targets that are in some stage of development. Another free goal!

Tell that resistance gremlin to take a nap.

The Instrument: You. Back to the Goals, Back to the Future

Personal Goals

Hey! You look like someone who wants to be reminded of something! I happen to have a reminder right here—this whole process is goal-driven. Go back to your goals. They tell you (at least) two things: what's emotionally important to you, and what it is you want to accomplish professionally. You can begin a useful instrument tuning right there. It isn't practical to hook each personal goal directly up with the characteristics of a potential target customer. Enrolling in a yoga class, or getting a new neck for your guitar, or taking a vacation may not have a direct business relation to targeted companies. (Unless perhaps yoga studios or travel agents are buyers of what you sell.)

I think of my business, to a large extent, in terms of how it enables me to fuel my emotional drivers, for myself and for my loved ones. For example, my business allows me to rent recording time in the best studios with the best engineers, and to hire and work with the best musicians this side of Saturn. It allows me to take vacations with my family. It allows me to *work* with my wife. My business is part of a mosaic that includes my loved ones and my loved pursuits. It feeds back on *all* aspects of my life. The more fulfilled I am emotionally, the more effective and enthusiastic a business-development instrument I become. It's a feedback loop. The point is, I'm very aware of the powerful integration of business to my personal goals. Going back to my personal goals and moving on them, bit by bit, sharpens me up and keeps me focused as a business-targeting instrument.

Professional Goals

Then there are the professional goals. They have a more down-to-earth and easier to see (but not more important!) connection to identifying and enhancing our characteristics as a targeting instrument. The professional goals might be thought of as the transformer of our inner drives into tangible results.

In our Chapter 1 example under Professional Goals (and the examples aren't pre-arranged illustrative set-ups! It's a coincidence that they help me make my point! I swear on a stack of *Selling from the Inside Out*!), there are items like: "Read *Power Point for Dummies*, and have two lunches (or breakfasts or dinners) with the president of the company and department heads during this year…" The idea is that we instinctively include professional goal items that will make us more effective business-developers. So it's logical that we start off with our goals when considering our characteristics as a targeting instrument. Our professional goals will tell us a lot about our current posture toward improved effectiveness, and might identify tools that we already possess and have at hand to help us.

The example goals also include (and this is probably a *must* goal) an annual income target. This goal is *really* (ready?) a hyper powerful, hyper accurate, easy-to-use guidance system for our targeting project. Does a prospect have characteristics that will help move us toward our income goal or not? It's a question we will continually ask as we pick through our net full of prospects. And a simple "Yes" or "No" is all that is needed.

The Chapter 1 professional goal example also touches an area that we'll explore more fully when we consider the total array of targets available to us (and it's just a *coincidence* that the example supports my thesis! I swear on a stack of my next book! [Watch your local newspaper for release announcements.]). There are valuable resources in our *past*, even in the pile of lost business and unsuccessful proposals. We have a bright future behind us.

The point is, now and forever, all along the Sales Process Map, we go back to our goals for guidance.

The Instrument: You. History

We all come from somewhere. So before we head out the door to land business, let's take some time to inventory the valuable experience we've accumulated over the years, perhaps without even knowing it. We'll assume that some of you have been working professionals for a while, perhaps with a variety of companies and perhaps in a variety of roles and fields. Others are just starting out on career paths. History is a good place to look for useful characteristics in either case. We'll start with those of us who have put a little mileage on the odometer already.

Remember, the job here is to take a little time to deepen our understanding of ourselves as targeting instruments. We throw a wide net—a wide net in time, and a wide net in space. Does the past throw any light on our characteristics? Let's take a look. We don't want to detour into a networking workshop. But let's take a little stroll down Memory Lane.

- *People*
Search back from the beginning of your working life. You don't have to go all the way back to your paper route or baby-sitting gigs, just back to your earliest recallable regular job. Don't try to remember everybody you ever encountered on that job. Just let your mind drift back, in a leisurely fashion, and see who emerges from the mist. We're looking for the energized ones, the ones who had a little something extra on the ball: customers, suppliers, bosses, parents, co-workers, and service providers. Those people in your life who had energy, imagination, leadership skills, and ethics. There won't be many of them. And I'm not talking about friends, unless they were energized friends. Jot the names down. And think back over faces from associations, committees, charitable organizations, bands, teams, and clubs. It's an inventory of the memorable (in a positive way) characters we've encountered over our career in our different roles. Use a yellow pad and #2 pencil.

- *Job Descriptions & Responsibilities*
  You're working in sales now, but what are you carrying forward from other professional lives? Have you been an office manager, an assembler, an IT specialist, a construction manager, a platoon commander, a long haul driver? On the list.

- *Memorable Deals*
  Any unusually complicated or nuanced or just plain big transactions that you found particularly exciting?

- *Special Projects*
  What have you done outside of your normal job description? Have you relocated offices and coordinated moves? Did you oversee the automation of an assembly process? Did you reorganize a sales department? Did you organize charitable drives? Did you work on special project committees? Yellow pad, #2.

- *Industries*
  What industries have you either worked in or supplied goods and services to? What industries provided goods and services to you? Jot them down.

- *Special Achievements*
  Have you earned awards or citations for extraordinary performance in sales or management? Or because you performed in some other noteworthy way?

What's the point of this exercise? In looking at ourselves as the instrumental component of a targeting process, we're starting off with the very broadest brush strokes in familiarizing ourselves with the equipment: ourselves. We're taking a professional inventory. We're reacquainting ourselves with where we've been, the experiences we've had, and the energetic peaks (in the form of people, projects and achievements) we've encountered. What does that do for us? At least four things:

1) Our history is a description of the journey that landed us where we are right now. A leisurely perusal of it gives us an appreciation of the depth and the richness of our own make-up. We tend to take ourselves for granted, or worse, we downgrade our skills, our experience. You're going to come through this little saunter with a greater appreciation of yourself. It's an energizing exercise. Guaranteed.

2) We might uncover some forgotten skill or experience that can be brought forward and that will have direct applicability in helping to differentiate us as sales people/service providers to certain business categories. This comes under the heading of "we don't even know what we know."

3) The process might inspire a few "where are they now?" searches. You can commit to tracking down a couple of interesting faces from the past as part of a short-term professional goal.

4) You may find hidden commonalities with co-workers.

Everybody, from the CEO on down, should keep a living sketch of his or her working history.

Are you reading this book while in the first six months of your first professional job? Don't worry. Take an inventory anyway. Go back through school, training, volunteer work, and travel. An important part of this exercise is to re-familiarize yourself with yourself. Maybe there are a few faces from school you might track down as a short-term goal. Your current employer has history you can appropriate. We'll look there next.

The Instrument: You. Your Expanded Corporate Presence

We've spent some time taking a historical look at ourselves as individuals. That, in turn, has highlighted our personal milestones and skill markers. Now we'll think in terms of our expanded selves within the corporate identity. This body has its own characteristics:

skills, experiences, successes, capabilities, history, culture, personality, and future. A little reminder: The purpose of this exercise is to both take a fresh look at all that we bring to the table as prospect-targeting instruments, and maybe to do a little instrument tuning along the way. This extended self, the corporate entity whose name is even bigger than ours on the business card—who is it? And how can it help us to help it as we sell and meet our goals?

We don't have to become experts in the minutiae of corporate history. But we're not taking anything for granted at this point. We want to step back and take a look at the total targeting package we're bringing to our prospect search. This includes ourselves *and* our employer. (In some cases, our self *is* our employer.) The package has to address a wide range of corporate types. Some of the ideas may not be particularly germane to your business, but bear with it; the overall process will be useful.

The Corporate Present

- The Sweet Spot

  What type and size account contributes the most to your company's achievement of objectives? Where are most of the company's customers located? Out of the range of goods and services that you offer, which are the best sellers? Which are the most profitable? Does your company do best with specific industry segments or types of individuals?

- *Services*

  What services are available to help you make a sale (e.g. financial analysis, presentation capabilities, factory tours, promotional materials, etc.)? What after-sale services are available to the customer? How is account management handled? What's the competition offering? What are the Top Ten reasons customers do business with your company?

The Corporate Future

Surprise! Let's look at goals. Maybe you work in a company that's very conscious of making sure that the sales people are constantly equipped with management's strategic outlook and the planned allocation of resources that will enable the company to stay in the game, strengthen its existing customer base, and predict and adjust to trends in the changing marketplace. Maybe management is keenly aware of your valuable front-line input on what's happening out there and what the competition is offering. In that type of environment, you can bring a sense of forward momentum to your targeting efforts. You might be able to see the potential for fulfilling needs that are a little bit down the road and might have remained invisible if you hadn't had proactive management that informs you of where they're going.

Ideally your company should set, and mark off, progress against goals, just like you're doing. (A company can even have "personal" goals, like becoming an attractive corporate neighbor, or providing a comprehensive health care plan, or sponsoring an employee arts program). Some of your professional goals could then be melded with corporate goals. For example, migration to a new industry segment.

The Corporate Past

Your company started somewhere (just like you), with a certain kind of customer base, and then, perhaps, grew and expanded over the years into different lines and services. Perhaps they were, or are, innovators in some striking way. Or maybe they're the bread and butter reliable, "not fancy, but you know what you're getting" type. Corporate history can be helpful in strengthening your connection to your environment and making you a more integrated, extended periscope when surveying the market.

It's also nice to know how you're perceived—whether there are favorable or perhaps unfair preconceptions about your corporation's abilities that *you* inherit as a salesperson. That kind of information might give you a leg up in evaluating the most likely prospects, or in preparing you to head off likely objections.

Time for some theatre:

Letting Your Hair Down with a Cutting-Edge Sales Manager

Reader of *Selling from the Inside Out*: I'm reading this really great book that encourages me to set goals and figure out who I am and who we are as a company, in order to help make me a more valuable salesperson going forward.

Sales Manager: And?

Reader: Well… I've done some digging through my past to get a clear look at my achievements and experience and strengths. I've got a good idea of what I want to accomplish, and I know what I have to do to get there. And I feel a fresh surge of energy! I'm taking a more focused approach to sales, concentrating my efforts on steps that will take me where I want to go and which, of course, will result in increased sales for the company. I'd like to get a better understanding of how you see things: how we got where we are, what our real strengths are, where you see the company going, where you see the market going… that sort of thing.

Sales Manager: We got here by selling forklifts to anybody who'll buy 'em. We stay here by selling forklifts to anybody who'll buy 'em. And we plan to continue selling forklifts to anybody who'll buy 'em. OK? Anything else? Go out and sell some forklifts.

The company you represent, with its characteristic history, its current strengths and weaknesses, and its future (goal-driven or not goal-driven), melds with you to form a unique targeting, prospecting, proposing and closing entity. Some businesses are extremely fluid and attuned to goal-setting (we mean goals outside of "just hit the numbers"; for instance, new market development, product innovation, improved customer service, retaining and attracting top talent and sales support). And some businesses are extremely rigid and aren't interested in tinkering with something that works well enough for the owners.

In either case, you, the sales professional, are best served by being goal-driven and focused. Don't tolerate a scatter-shot or less than clear approach to your livelihood anymore; it's too shaky a foundation for something this important. If you find you are more goal-driven than your employer, then, when you're having lunch with the president, ask her what her plans for future development look like. She'll probably be glad you asked, and if not, it might get her thinking. And don't forget to yellow pad some notes on what you find out in your corporate inventory.

The Targets

We've thought about the targeting instrument, namely ourselves and ourselves combined with an extended corporate body. We've taken a look at the features of the instrument (personal and corporate) and inventoried distinguishing characteristics. Now we turn our attention to the targets. We're going to take a similar approach, big picture to little picture; past, present and future.

An Interlude: Thinking Great Thoughts

I remember looking out of the window from the fifty-third floor of a Manhattan skyscraper and remarking to a colleague, "Just look. Think about all of the people out there who have never even heard of us!" I think she said something like, "Huh?" You (the reader) might be saying to yourself, "For a guy who's always harping about specificity, how can he get all charged up by looking out a window and thinking about the ten million people who have never heard of him? That's a weird kind of zeroing-in." You'd be right in pointing that out to me and entitled to one-quarter of a point toward a "Most Alert Reader" merit badge. But allow me to indulge myself.

There was something empowering about looking out that window. It was a sense of abundance. The sidewalks and streets and office buildings and hotels and buses and taxis and apartment buildings and delis were just teeming with people. People who didn't even know I existed. What enormous opportunity! I'd probably had my attention buried in a sales presentation, obsessively chasing a rabbit into a warren, when suddenly I lifted my head. And there it was: the whole world. It got me out of myself and made me feel a sense of limitless possibility. It was a good feeling. It's good to lift your head up from time to time. There's a lot of unexplored world waiting for you. And Manhattan has no lock on abundance. The unlimited supply of prospects, of opportunities, is everywhere.

OK. Let's focus.

From the Limitless to Something We Can Handle

When I started in the insurance business, I had a hard and fast rule: *If it had a working smokestack, I went after it.* After all, *They buy insurance, just not from us yet!* Upon further reflection, I don't think I even cared if it was a *working* smokestack, and I'm not positive if I always knew that there was actually a "they" there. When I started my sales consulting business and was trying to get the thing off the ground, I thought I was much more disciplined. If someone, anyone, would agree to meet with me, and they had two employees (making them *twice* my size), they were targets. Oh, those days when we had no customers!

Today, when that same prospect calls, the impulse to buy a plane ticket passes quickly. This process is one of the mistakes that Tom Redmond made that you do not have to make. Now that my business is up and running, I want to pass on to you the benefit of what I've learned about the process of selecting worthy targets.

Let's position ourselves on the Sales Process Map. We're on the square that reads "Target Accounts." We're going to include the next square, which reads "Target Account Research," at the end of the chapter. We've looked at the targeting instruments, ourselves and our extended corporate selves. Now we're going to gather a group of prospects, and finally we'll sift through that first group by doing some verification.

The First Catch: Using Gut Instinct and Experience

If we throw the widest possible net for prospects, we get some very big catches. Too big. The universe is awesome and inspiring. The millions of people viewed from a fifty-third story window are awesome and inspiring. But, going back to a previous thought, we have to get to "tiny" and inspiring before we have an actionable idea. There are a number of easily accessible tools to help us with our first pass at the limitless opportunities out there. We're going to handle these tools with "guided gut instinct and experience" in order to cut the universe down to a manageable size.

Gut instinct and experience may sound like fairly blunt guiding tools. But they're not as blunt as they were before our little personal and corporate stock-taking exercises. Writing our findings down on that yellow pad with a #2 pencil helped bond them to our way of seeing ourselves in relation to the world of possibility. Gut instinct and experience are powerful and hard-earned tools. Don't underestimate them. They're not vague and amorphous, especially when hooked up to some more precision accessories. Remember, we're cutting down the field here, not trying to find the needle in the haystack.

Here are some accessories we can hook up to our instinct and experience:

For the Present

- *Goals*

Let's first stop off at (you guessed it) our goals, specifically our year-end W-2 number. Look back at the Chapter 1 example. We've figured out how many new business meetings we need per month in order to hit our number. A few steps earlier, we'd determined an average sale amount. We have to spend our meetings, proposals and calls wisely in order to stay on track to our year-end number.

Key questions for you: Does a company buy enough of what you sell to justify spending energy in their direction? Can they possibly help you to your goal? Yes/No? Go with your gut and experience. It's not OK to "make a sale, *any* sale." In my own case, I can no longer afford (nor could I ever afford) to consider accounts that don't meet a certain minimum dollar threshold. If I don't discipline myself in that regard, then my business can't do its job in nourishing the lives of our clients, the lives of my loved ones, and my life. We're all infinitely better off taking a pass on a tempting but distracting morsel, and spending that energy in the arena dictated by my goals.

On the other hand, I feel your pain; the pain, the pressure to make a sale, any sale; the pressure of at least having something on the board that you're working on. The discipline needed here to turn business away is almost, quite frankly, out of the reach of normal mortals. You will work on business that does not meet your criteria, you will be disappointed, and you will make mistakes that Tom Redmond made that you do not have to make.

But you will stop making these mistakes. Why? Because you will follow a systematic process to bring business in the door. You will measure your results, you will make course corrections, and you will have more business to work on than you can handle. Your fear will dissolve when you are loaded up with prospects and clients, and you will reach your goals faster.

- *Size, industry, expectations of the prospect*

How does the prospect match up with the "sweet spot" of your company? Are they way larger than your typical customer? Are they in an industry where you have a big following? Does the level of customer service you provide match, or is it better than what they're used to?

- *Location*

  Is there a decision-maker within reasonable traveling distance so that you can maintain adequate face-to-face contact, and keep an eye on account management? Or do distance and face-to-face communication matter?

- *Health*

  Do you get a sinking feeling that a prospect is struggling to survive? Or does this matter? Perhaps you can provide a solution for them.

From the Past

- *Lost business and unsuccessful proposals*

  Write up a list of lost customers and companies to which you've made unsuccessful presentations over the last two years. These are prospects that you know a lot about. Count on it that something has changed in their market, the economy, their relationships, etc. Subject them to the same criteria we outlined above. There is likely to be some low-hanging fruit here.

Into the Future

- *Referrals*

  Take a look at referral sources. Every industry segment which is close to your initial "sweet spot" is swimming in service providers: suppliers, accountants, and lawyers, for starters. Subject your referral prospects to "guided gut" evaluation, as above. Are they really active players? Are they inclined to work with you in building a mutually beneficial network? Don't forget trade associations and trade magazines. Are they worth cultivating? Are they proactive on behalf of their industry? Are they accessible?

SELLING FROM THE INSIDE OUT

Confidence and Energy

Einstein taught us that matter and energy are equivalent. Confidence and energy are equivalent too. (Where's my Nobel Prize?) We've become reacquainted with our targeting equipment and have made a "first cut" evaluation of targets. How do we bring these things together? What's the unifying principle? Confidence. When we look at a prospect from where we sit now, are we confident that we have the background to make a credible pitch, and the equipment to land the business? Are we confident that we have the resources to service the business once we get it? Are we confident that the account fits the profile of what *we* require to get to our goals?

Confidence energizes. When we overlay our characteristics as targeters with the characteristics of prospects, we find certain resonances, good places to look for success. It's another one of those darned feedback loops: confidence becomes energy becomes enthusiasm becomes inspiration becomes new ideas becomes success becomes confidence—it never ends. Not to mention confidence's impact on our personal goals, which affect our... (you get the picture).

Target Account Research/Verification

We're still in the situation room. We're not ready to go out just yet. The effort we've put into pulling together a group of first-cut worthy targets deserves some refining, some verification before we go any further along the Sales Process Map. Call it a gut check. Today's salesperson has an enormous amount of resources at his disposal for advancing the refining process before heading out the door on a sales call. We've gathered a group of prospects. We want to verify that more than our intuition is on the right track.

We can check a website to get a feel for the image that the company sets forth and the direction in which they say they're heading. There are industry specific directories and general business directories that can help us to understand a company's size, structure, products and growth pattern. If your company doesn't own the directories, they're available at the local library and online. Google the prospect and find out if there's any recent buzz that might be useful. If they're in the neighborhood, take a drive by and see if the parking lot's full. We're not out to write a detailed report on each prospect, but a little preparation might save us the trouble of soliciting a company that's on the verge of bankruptcy. (Wait until *after* they go bankrupt; then they become a court-ordered good customer.) We're zeroing in. A final take on the landing area might help us determine whether it's a worthy destination.

(Your Name), Inc. Sales Process

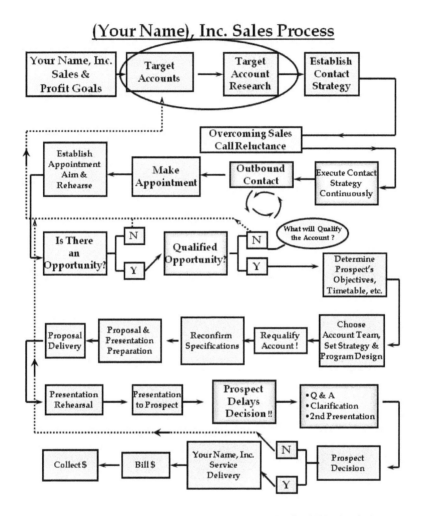

Copyright ©Redmond Group, Inc. 2011

Chapter 3

CONTACT STRATEGY
Who, Why and Why Not?

It's time to stay seated. And it's OK if you're getting anxious to run out the door and pull down some big sales. That's a good sign. But our job is to show you how to construct and get the most energy out of your value-enhancing sales producing machine.

Maybe it's a good time to underscore some fundamental notions behind our approach. We're developing a personalized *process*. It's a proven way to become more valuable to yourself and *everyone* who enters your sphere of influence, in and outside of business. The process ensures that your sphere of influence will grow. Your professional competition will notice this growth because customers will start to disappear from *their* gravitational field. That's life in a tough universe. If your competition is in the vicinity of your expanding galaxy, then they're going to lose some stars.

Ours is a basic, building-block approach. Once we've gone through the process together, you'll end up with something like an assembly line that runs 24/7. It's automated, efficient, and productive even when you're not tending to it. The process turns out professional and personal successes at the end of the line, which are re-invested in the system. It's a co-generation plant, producing confidence/energy as a by-product that's fed back.

We're not dealing in one-shot sales gimmickry or slogans or tricks. We're building a plant, from the bottom up, on a fundamental, proven plan, with custom-fit features supplied by your unique background and personal and professional goals. Once it's up and running, it has permanence. Right now we're building. Stick with it and, square by square, brick by brick, you'll have constructed something that's as close to a perpetual-motion machine as nature allows. It creates its own momentum. It's a closed system.

If you hit a wall in the process, the Sales Process Map will show you where to go to free up the snag. Prospects are cycled through the Sales Process Map until you land the account, or resend the prospect through the process, or determine that the prospect gets set aside, maybe for future cycling. Remember the "Rolling 106" in Chapter 2? This is it—a consistently-sized, permanent inventory of prospects built and maintained over time.

We've established our goals and organized them into a follow-up structure. We've taken a close look at the instrument (you) that's going to be activated in the service of targeting (ourselves and our expanded, corporate selves), and we've thrown a big net to gather in the widest array of targets. Now we'll examine the issues surrounding the establishment of contact with the targets.

Your prospects have many skills. Hiring you is not one of them. But they're teachable. Acquiring new customers is a pro-active endeavor. Ironically, once the Sales Process Map has become second nature in your day-to-day business conduct, you'll find that your referral business grows to become the largest source of new opportunity. Pro-activity will morph into an increasingly receptive mode. That's where we want to go. We want business to knock at *our* door. At the Redmond Group, referrals constitute by far the largest percentage of new business. We had to build to this point, and the Sales Process Map got us here. Even if a prospect comes walking through our door, pre-sold on us, guess where they go? That's right! They go to the "Goals" square. They have to fit *our* profile, they have to help us reach *our* goals.

The Big Picture

Let's start with an overview of the Contact Strategy landscape. Then we'll look at how we might cut the field down to size. There are two extremes on the prospect contact spectrum, and representatives of each extreme have one of several names:

- At one end: the Ice Queen, Absolute Zero, the Abominable Snowman, Nanook of the North, Deep Freeze, and the Penguin. These are people who are responsible for buying what you sell at companies that fit your goal requirements and fall within your target range. They've never heard of you, or your company. They're the coldest of cold calls, but it's a call you've thought about and figured that it's worth making. As far as you can tell, you'd like to do business with them.

- Those at the other end of the spectrum also have names: Pre-Cooked, Just Add Invoice, Hot Stuff, Burning Man, Boiling Point, Hot Tamale, and Greased Lightning. These are people who just can't wait to see you because so-and-so has told them that they can't consider themselves true professionals unless they've given you a big order. They realize that their lives are empty without you. They want to know if it's possible to pre-pay for several years' worth of product. *They* call *you* to find out the most convenient times for a meeting, and they ask what kind of restaurant *you* like best. On the first call, which *they* initiate, they want to know your birth sign and the names of your pets. (It can get a little creepy; sometimes one might prefer the Ice Queen.) Your job at this end of the spectrum is to slow them down enough to determine whether they can help you reach *your* goal. And to reassure them that you'll find a place for their order (if they're qualified).

So what's the highest quality, biggest-return way to manage this huge spectrum?

Cutting the Big Picture Down to Size

Let's assume that you're the most charming, informed, quick-thinking, smoothest cold-caller of all time. You know all of the techniques for getting the buyer on the phone and landing that face-to-face meeting. You're a regular Clint Eastwood or Annie Oakley —nobody stands a chance. Buyers melt at the sound of your voice.

We're not denigrating those skills. We should all sharpen our cold-calling techniques. Some may have natural talents, and *all* can benefit from a focus on skill development. Effective calling can be learned, practiced, and improved. Chapter 5 will be devoted to "How to Make an Appointment." But there's some prep work that can be very useful in helping us set the table for getting the most out of our contact opportunities, no matter how sharp we are already.

A Number's a Number's a Number. Or Is It?

You'll often hear that sales is a "numbers game." To some extent, we agree. After all, we use the word "number" in our key mantra: "Sales success rests upon the *number* of *contacts* initiated with prospective buyers on a consistent basis." But there are big qualitative differences in the ways of looking at numbers.

On one end of the scale is "dialing for dollars." This approach involves getting a list of names (perhaps even semi-qualified) and making as many calls as possible with a standard pitch, hoping that by "saturation bombing" you actually land a meeting or two. You might hit a buyer who happens to pick up the phone and likes the sound of your voice, or one who's looking forward to next week's vacation and feels peculiarly receptive to a cheery cold-caller. Maybe you even hit someone who's ready to buy what you're selling. After all, it's a big world, with a lot of serendipitous convergences. (I begged my editor to keep this phrase in—Victory!)

Let's imagine the human nature of a prospect who's in the "cold" range of our selected targets and see if "dialing for dollars" works for us, or for the prospect.

- From a prospective buyer's point of view, the world is swimming in vendors and service providers, some of whom they're already working with, and most of whom (including you) they might be perfectly content never to meet.

- Like all of us, the prospect experiences an overwhelming "noise" level on a daily basis. Put yourself in her shoes. She has an important responsibility to acquire the best goods and services available to her jurisdiction, at the best price. The job also involves negotiating contracts and managing vendor relationships. She's swamped in unsolicited pitches from would-be providers on a daily basis. She's heard and seen it all.

- She (like everyone else) has to contend with internal managerial and political chaos that often seems more overwhelming than the daily assaults by vendors.

- She has a life, believe it or not, outside of sitting through presentations by hopeful sellers. Her husband's building a giant balsa wood replica of Godzilla in the dining room, and her daughter just had her nose pierced (for the third time) against orders. On the plus side, her women's reading club is going great, notwithstanding the fact that they never talk about books, just husbands, ex-husbands, and children. She never brings up the subject of hiring you.

The cold end of the spectrum is the most challenging. And, you guessed it; it's also the biggest piece of the pie. There are, by far, more worthy prospective targets who *don't* know you than who *do* know you. Someday (sooner than you think) you're going to meet most of your goals through referrals. But you're going to get there by starting in the daunting, nutrient-rich depths of the not-yet-known. That's where we started. That's where the treasure is hidden.

So, imagine that this capable, resilient and sometimes beleaguered woman winds up in your "dialing for dollars" crosshairs. What are the chances that you make a beneficial contact?

From her perspective:

• You're indistinguishable from the multitude of your competitors. Even if you're a "top gun" solicitor with quality product, you need a perfect alignment of the stars to get her on the phone and make her think, "I've just *got* to meet this person!"

• You're only adding to the noise in her life by winging it with a canned call. If you're lucky, she'll forget you. If she remembers you, you'll be in a worse position than if she'd never heard of you at all.

• The (short) time she spends with you is a fruitless detour from her other concerns, both job-related and personal. She doesn't need that. She's not an enemy.

From your perspective:

• You spent a valuable shot on a worthy target, with an infinitesimally small probability of hitting the mark.

• You neither honored your energy resources or her energy resources, setting both of you back. You have a failed call without the satisfaction of having given it your best shot. She's had to fight off a random-sounding pitch. Setbacks can't be entirely avoided, but they accumulate. We want to get to a place where our efforts are worthy of us *and* our prospect.

That doesn't add up to a great list.

So how *do* we navigate the icy waters of cold calls? When in doubt, look at the Sales Process Map. Remember, we're building a permanent, value-enhancing, sales producing machine from the ground up. It turns out that we can set our contact strategy firmly on top of the previous square, Targeting Accounts. We'll use a grounded and guided approach to sorting out the number of contacts. Only top-quality numbers on the Sales Process Map—no more scatter-shots allowed.

Getting Warm

How do we impose quality control on a numbers game? We start by seeing if it's possible to change some stone-cold calls into warm calls.

From Square One, Goal Setting, we've been working with the notion that we are points in a web of relationships. We're not isolated "work units." Work is part of an integrated system that includes our personal world. Our personal and professional lives, in turn, have their own networks. The written goal-setting discipline brings to the surface the energy that runs through our *entire* lives, our *entire* web of relationships. So?

In Targeting Accounts, we spent time getting familiar with and honing our targeting instrument—us. We looked backward and forward to re-familiarize ourselves with the experience we've picked up, the faces we've met, and the direction in which we're headed. We did the same thing with our extended, corporate selves. Now we can lower Contact Strategy right on top of that foundation and "see what we can see" from our new perch.

It's time for a clumsy analogy. Imagine standing ten feet away from your spouse, girlfriend, boyfriend, friend, or child. This probably won't work with pets, although it's possible that it works with very smart (and strong) chimpanzees. You're facing your partner, and each of you has a golf ball in your hand. You (gently!) lob the golf ball toward your partner (he does the same) and try to get the balls to collide in mid-air. Although we've never actually executed this thought-experiment, it's reasonable to assume that on an overwhelming number of tosses, the balls would sail by each other, making no contact.

Now each of you picks up a golf bag (assume you've been bulking up at the gym). The golf bag is loaded with balls, tees, and clubs. Each of you tosses a full bag toward the other. There's a much greater chance that the bags will collide in mid-air and, if not, that in the pile of equipment that now lies between you, something from one bag has made contact with something from the other bag. Clumsy enough?

The point is that one isolated unit (solicitor) trying to make contact with another isolated unit (solicited) is a very low-percentage shot, even for the best sharpshooter. But a web of relationships (which, in fact, is what we *really* are) making contact with another web of relationships (which, in fact, is what everyone else *really* is) has a much higher probability of occurring. In the previous chapter, we've already done the work in figuring out the dimensions and characteristics of our extended-web selves (as individuals and parts of a corporate body). Let's apply that work to contact strategy.

Pre-Sorting

We're looking at a group of desirable but cold targets. We want to warm them up. Sift them through our individual inventory (last chapter). There's a list of people we've known (co-workers and service providers [lawyers and accountants]), jobs and responsibilities we've held, deals we've negotiated, special projects we've worked on, and industries we've become familiar with through suppliers. Do we see anything that might jibe with the characteristics of our cold prospect? Remember, we've done some target research already, so look back on it. Do any resonances emerge? We can always zero in a little more and do some additional target research. Who are the target's lawyers? What trade associations do they belong to? Who are their major suppliers? Send that resistance gremlin out on an errand.

Then there's our corporate body. Does the prospect hit our corporate sweet spot in a way that might raise our profile as a supplier? Are they part of an industry in which our company has established a track record? Is there noteworthy corporate history that might be germane to their particular situation? Is our company heading in certain directions that might be of special interest to the prospect?

To pound the point home, we're a big web of relationships and they're a big web of relationships. A little bit of digging (much of which we've already done) can turn a random, cold shot into a welcome, warm handshake:

- We can distinguish ourselves from our competitors. Maybe we can uncover a beneficial commonality. Or we might get an introduction through a common acquaintance whom we've discovered by doing a little research. Perhaps we've seen a fit between a new product and the target's strategic direction.

- We rise above the noise.

- We give proper respect to our energy (we don't waste what we've developed) and we respect the energy of the prospect (we have a substantial reason for calling).

You might be saying to yourself, "So you're talking about research and networking. What's the big deal? Everybody knows about research and networking." You get one-half a point toward your "Worthy Critic" merit badge for that observation.

But what we're aiming to accomplish here is more than a suggestion that you try to network your way into meetings. There can still be a "me against the world" flavor to thinking of networking as a separate tool that you may or may not pick up and use. *We want to develop a habitual way of seeing ourselves as part of an integrated whole.* Networking should occur as a natural outgrowth of who we really are (a node in a web of relationships), who other people really are (nodes in webs of relationships), and what *our* goals are, and what *they* want to accomplish.

By the way, remember last chapter when we pointed out that doing an inventory might turn up similarities in our individual experiences with those of other members of our sales team? If you work as part of a sales team, and you've all followed the Sales Process Map to this point, you might find a big increase in your collective reach. Do the sifting together. You might be pleasantly surprised at the benefits: an enhanced chance at cold business, greater team cohesion, and confidence.

The pre-sorting process produces another side benefit. It sets us down the path to referral development. Let's say we think that a previous business relationship is someone who might have some useful insight into the nature of a cold prospect's needs. In making that "face from the past" call, we might actually gather some useful information. But we'll *definitely* re-open a door that might someday lead to a benefit.

The resistance gremlin says, "I'd rather just get on the phone and start banging away. This sounds like too much homework." Contact with a prospect is a pivotal point of passage on the Sales Process Map. As we become more valuable, crucial thresholds carry more freight. There's no longer such a thing as "tossing off" a call. The energy that goes into Contact Strategy should be worthy of all that we bring to the table as individuals and as parts of a corporate body, *and* of all the mutual benefits that result from a successful relationship with a new customer.

Then What?

We've tried to convert cold prospects into slightly warmer prospects. But for most of them, maybe all, we couldn't find a way to heat them up. Was that a waste of time? And what do we do now?

It wasn't a waste of time on at least four counts.

1) Every time we make the effort to look at ourselves and our companies in light of the perceived needs of a prospect, we see something new. We're constantly learning and picking up fresh information about ourselves and the market. New prospects give us the opportunity to surface knowledge we don't even know we know. The process has a cumulative effect.

2) Our companies are constantly changing, adding new customers in new segments, adding new products, developing new strategic paths. Our prospecting strategies will help us to be more informed, fresher representatives of our employers.

3) The energy spent in trying to make each call count comes back to us. It's not forever lost, like a hip-shot, even if we don't find a way in on the first pass. For example, we've re-awakened some old relationships and established new ones while digging for referrals. That's reusable energy, lying there for us to tap it again.

4) And don't believe that you and your team don't have the time to devote to a little inventory and pre-screening before plunging into a cold phone call or e-mail. It's like saying a surgeon doesn't have time to look at an x-ray before she starts operating. If you look back over the time-allocation/reward ratio for a random approach to cold prospects, you'll see some *real* wastage. A nervous impulse to "do something… anything!" is a wheel-spinning fast track to the noisy horde. You're too valuable for that.

What Do We Do Now?

We take those choice, but still cold prospects and put them under the microscope. We're going to give them the special attention they deserve. You'll be interested to know that Chapter 4 will be on the subject of blocks and call reluctance. Chapter 5 addresses the art of landing an appointment.

Contact: Different Objectives and Different Tools

The general concept of "contact" covers a lot of territory. We've talked about initial, door-opening contact in the form of a call, and we're going to spend more time in that arena. It's a rich and challenging territory.

Advertising and Public Relations

There are other ways in which contact is made between you and the world of prospects—for example, advertising and public relations. These are generally avenues for your corporate body to be presented to the outside world, although public relations can be tailored to the level of the individual. You might not have much influence over advertising expenditures or placement, especially in a large company. But you should make an effort to keep up with the direction and development of themes in ad campaigns.

Ad campaigns are long-distance, background "warm ups," and you shouldn't ever find yourself knowing less about what your ads are saying than a prospect knows. If you work in a smallish company, try to talk the advertising manager into placing ads in trade magazines that are of particular interest to your business development plans, especially if you're cultivating an expertise in an exciting growth area. Keep hounding him! If one of your personal goals involves community or charitable volunteer work, then prepare a PR release describing the activities of your project and submit it to your communications department.

Alternative Warm-Ups

There are a variety of ways in which an astute salesperson can try to transform a cold prospect into a warmer prospect:

- Distinguish yourself from the competition by reading trade magazines and becoming an expert in trends and issues that face a particular industry. You might very well discover an opportunity to offer a product or service that illuminates your extra degree of initiative. At a minimum, you'll demonstrate a greater interest in the prospect's business than is typically demonstrated by the average "let me tell you about *me*" sales person.

- Attend trade shows and introduce yourself to the representative of a prospective customer. Describe your service and ask for help in navigating their company. But *don't* overstay your welcome if he's trying to attend to paying customers. He'll appreciate your savvy.

Contact Maintenance

Once you've gotten in front of a prospect and they're either an active customer or a work in progress, there are a variety of ways to maintain contact and provide useful information (hint—place one of the following on your professional goals list):

- First of all—this is not a suggestion—fully commit to using some type of Prospect Management Software. Tools of wonderment—they can do way more than you need.

- Newsletters, either e-mail or hard copy. Short and punchy with an interesting bit of relevant news. *Don't* send to people you've never met; you'll qualify as first-rate noise.

- Teleconferences, conference calls or "webinars" to review your product or service delivery, to listen to suggestions from various departments, to plan future actions and schedule follow-ups.

- Live seminars. Schedule a presentation on a subject of particular interest to buyers of your product. This *is* an appropriate invitation for potential customers whom you've never met.

• Social media—New tools have appeared in your contact toolkit, like LinkedIn, Facebook, Twitter, etc. This segment is developing too fast to figure out—just keep moving in this direction and use these services in tandem with the other contact maintenance methods.

• Offer to write an interesting and relevant article in a trade magazine for a prospect's industry. The subject has to be more interesting than how great *you* are. Don't worry, the byline alone is a bucket's worth of PR. And you can mail out reprints.

• Write a book. Don't laugh. *I* wrote a book. OK, now you can laugh.

• **Radical Notion #1**: Did we mention that a phone call from time to time could be helpful?!

• Personal notes and even (dare we say) actual letters on your actual company stationery. The one thing we're quite sure of is that the U.S. Postal Service is still working—your letter will get through.

• Telepathy. Send brain-waves to prospects at various times of the day or night, instructing them to call you and place an order. Or rather, plant a rumor with your competition that telepathy works. Hey, that sounds like a great book title: *Sales by Telepathy—Never Having to Make Another Outbound Contact.* Stay tuned.

The simple point is this. Contact strategy encompasses initial encounters with prospects, *and* ongoing sales and relationship maintenance.

Pre-Warmed Relationships

In our targeting exercises, we stepped back and inventoried our past. There are customers that we no longer have (including those from previous professional lives), and presentations that we've made and failed to get the business. We already know a lot about these companies, and perhaps we've got some friends on-board. Count on this—something has changed at the prospect or in the economy or in their market. *Things change.* And they change fast.

We once announced to a prospect, the day after we'd been in-formed of a second-place finish, "Welcome to the re-solicitation of your account!" That's an attitude they don't hear every day of the week. And it can be presented in a non-annoying manner. People are generally impressed (or at least amused) with that kind of dog-gedness.

Referrals

We want to get to the point where most of our business comes through referrals. Think of contacting referral sources with the same kind of forethought that you apply to direct customers. The best referral source of all is going to be the customers you gain by employing the Sales Process Map, square by square.

Let's get rid of those blocks and resistors that are still hanging around.

> From our Sales Coach Newsletter:
> "I never met a referral that I didn't like," by Anonymous.

In our constant search for the easy way to sell (there is no easy way, but we continue to look), one consistent factor is that the most successful sales organizations are aware of their numbers and make course corrections by them. Organizational and individual patterns of success can be duplicated, and challenges recognized and overcome. Do you know your referral ratio?

When it comes to referrals, we advise our clients to think of themselves as sales managers. That's right; your clients now work for you! How are you managing and leading your clients, prospects, network, etc. in delivering referrals to you? Of your current prospects, how many came as a result of a referral? If your referral ratio is below 60%, what can be done to improve it?

Here's what we know:

- Referrals are the best way to generate new business and expand your prospecting network. We estimate that hit ratios from referred prospects start at 50% and go up from there.

- Set referral goals: How many referrals can be generated for the balance of this year? Okay, how about for next month? Next quarter? Your assignment is to pick a number and write it down.

- Target your referral sources. You know that your products and services are terrific. Where is the greatest level of personal trust between you and your client? Which customers are the safest to ask? Think of those clients who have actually experienced and recognized your outstanding service. Who comes to mind? This is where to begin. Start from the possible and move gradually toward the impossible.

- Ask. Yes, that's all there is to it—just ask. We recommend that you even set goals with your referral sources. Here's a dialogue example: "I'm building my business and would value your assistance. Is it possible to obtain five referrals/introductions from you over the next three months?" Your assignment is to develop and practice your own dialogue.

- Be specific as to the types of referrals you are seeking. Targeting specific accounts, individuals or industry niches will be helpful to your referral source. Ask for and discuss specific strategies for reaching each referral.

- Explain the process: how you will communicate, offer outstanding value, and gracefully walk away if you are not the right fit or the best solution.

- Upon conclusion of the activity with the referred account, thank your referral source again (and ask for another!)

Insurance industry studies have shown that over 90% of those asked are happy to refer business. That's the good news. The bad news is that less than 3% are asked for referrals. Sometimes we simply expect that a satisfied client will naturally offer business contacts—stop that thinking immediately! You need to ask.

We always feel good about ourselves when we refer business contacts to others. Let your clients and referral sources feel good about themselves. Why not ask for a referral today? How about one by 5 pm?

(Your Name), Inc. Sales Process

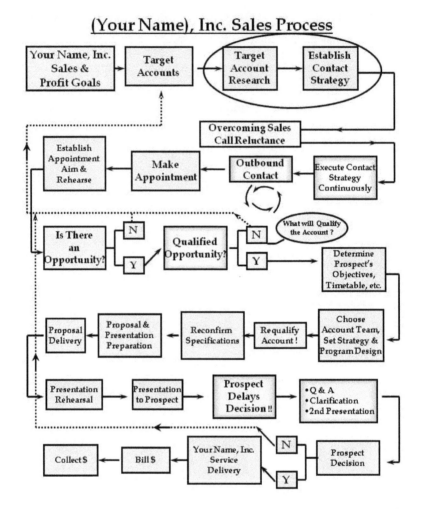

Copyright ©Redmond Group, Inc. 2011

Chapter 4

CALL RELUCTANCE
Why I Won't Do This Stuff

Picture this—circa 1992 in my office at my high-paying, prestigious job. I was not only managing a group of extraordinarily successful, experienced and highly charged producers, but I was also producing business. My personal objective was to have 16 new commercial business appointments per month, and it took me 156 contacts to get to that level. The only reason I knew these numbers is that I used a prospect management system that would track the outbound contacts I was making. One of the more interesting functions was that I would click on someone's name and his or her phone would ring.

Speaking of phones ringing, my phone rang and my life changed. The person calling said, "Hello, Tom, this is so and so, and you have sales call reluctance." That was her pitch, nothing else. I responded with something stupid (OK, make that arrogant) like, "Oh no, no, I'm the best at this! I get 16 appointments per month, and it takes me 156 contacts to get them. I have no call reluctance."

"Yes, you do."

"No, I don't."

"Yes, you do."

"No, I don't, to infinity."

She finally suggested that I take an assessment tool called SPQ*GOLD®—The Call Reluctance® Scale. And if I liked the results, maybe I would buy some—this one was on the house. How could she be denied? I took the assessment. At that time, the Internet was still in its early days, so the assessment wasn't even online; I filled out the form, faxed it in and met with her to review my individual results. *And my life changed!* The results were absolutely right on. It found my sales call reluctance. Reaching way back and finding some rare humility, I remember saying, "How did it know?" It was that powerful, that robust. Stay tuned for more about the discovery of my specific call reluctance tendencies.

I then decided that my sales team should take the same assessment. Not only did we discover individual call reluctance tendencies in the producers, but we also found a pattern of all reluctance within the team. And this was shocking: the team's pattern included my own sales call reluctance. I was teaching my team how *not* to make outbound contacts! So call reluctance behaviors are catching; I learned mine from others and I was passing mine on—I was contagious!

Fast forward a few years, and upon leaving that company and my high-paying, prestigious job behind, I decided that this call reluctance assessment should become a very important part of my new career and our new practice. I earned the certification as a call reluctance instructor, and here we are years later—mission accomplished. Overcoming sales call and contact reluctance has become a major part of our work.

How did this really begin? Well, I may have a fact or two wrong here, but you'll get the spirit of the evolution of Call Reluctance... at least, this is how I explain it to our prospects and clients. Back in 1979 a major company in the financial services industry, specifically, life insurance, made this observation:

"80% of our salespeople are failing."

And as a former sales manager, I would have to say that this is called "Welcome to Sales Hell."

"How's it going?"
"Oh, only 80% of my salespeople are failing."
"Sounds like Sales Hell to me."

So the senior folks at this company decided they'd better check this out and actually do something about it. So they hired a couple of psychologists, George Dudley and Shannon Goodson. George and Shannon got to work interviewing people, researching the data, and looking for common characteristics of the 20% who were successful and the 80% that were failing.

Although I don't know this for a fact, I have this vision of George and Shannon going back to the senior managers at their client and saying something like, "We have the answer—we know why 80% are failing and only 20% are succeeding." Of course, the senior managers say, "Tell us, tell us!" And George says, "Pay us first, because you will not believe our answer." So they got paid, and the answer was:

"The only significant difference found between the 80% who failed and the 20% who succeeded was that the 20% made more contacts. That's the only difference."

When you think about it, here's a company with specific product lines and service offerings that were understood by the sales teams, who targeted prospective accounts in particular identified territories with precise characteristics, supported by company-wide sales training programs with a company-wide sales process, combined with a structure of mentors, coaches, sales managers and sales leaders (they even had an annual sales conference, but only for the 20%, of course). And yet, why did 80% of the team fail to make more contacts?

Can you begin to relate to this? Isn't it true that you have specific products and services that are understood by you and your sales teams, who target prospective accounts in particular identified territories with precise characteristics, supported by internal and external sales training programs, sales process and maybe even a structure of mentors, coaches, sales managers and sales leaders? And yet, what is blocking you from making more contacts? What about just that next contact? Why is your team hesitating with the next outbound contact?

So, George and Shannon began their pursuit of studying the 80%, and that's how this Call Reluctance practice was born.

One comment as to why I made this commitment to the Call Reluctance practice. There were remedies available, counter measures that could be applied to help us to overcome this phenomenon. Quite frankly, if there were no counter measures available, I was not interested in moving forward.

The way call reluctance works is like this: I don't know about you, but there's this internal voice, this internal dialogue that says something like, "I've got to contact Joe Jones, but no, I think I'll go do something else first."

Think about this for yourself. During the past week, can you honestly say that you contacted every one of the prospects (or clients) that you've been meaning to contact? Or did you go and do something else? OK, how about this—did you see any of your colleagues hesitate to contact a prospect?

There are sixteen reasons why this happens, sixteen reasons why we are transported away from initiating outbound contacts. In our practice, we're really quite neutral about the mechanism for making those contacts—is it using the phone, e-mail, social media, working the room at a networking event, harvesting referrals from existing clients, walk-ins, cold calls, pre-approach letters sent via conventional mail services? The one common factor has to be *initiating the* outbound *contact*.

WARNING: Call Reluctance/Contact Reluctance is not to be confused with the normal routines of responding to an inbound call, following up on needed information, answering a routine client question, or ordering a pizza. These responses are important in day-to-day work with clients, but we are compelled to hammer this home one more time—it is all about *initiating the outbound contact for purposes of ethical self-promotion* (more on that in a bit; please keep reading). This reluctance blocks us from executing on this difficult and yet absolutely critical aspect of our jobs as sales professionals. We can also be blocked at networking events or professional conferences where we find ourselves hanging out with our pals as opposed to working the room, where there are real live walking and talking opportunities all around us.

So where did this all come from? First, the good news here is that call reluctance is not some type of character flaw. Call reluctance is something that we were taught, something we learned and probably observed over the years. One more time: call reluctance is not some type of character flaw. Phew, that's a relief! One of the most interesting aspects of this work is that we can find ourselves thinking of these tendencies as qualities. I like to think of them now as "qualities gone bad!"

We need to pause here and gratefully acknowledge the enormous contribution that George, Shannon and their team at Behavioral Sciences Research Press made in transforming not only my own career, but the careers of millions of salespeople around the globe—those sales professionals who took this assessment, seriously followed up with the necessary work, and became more valuable than they already were. We want to give full acknowledgement of their contribution and are happy to report that they gave us permission to devote a chapter to this topic. We are very grateful for that on so many levels.

I would also like to gratefully acknowledge the thousands of men and women in the business of sales who took the leap, took the risk of participating in this critical analysis, and put their trust in me. We have been able to offer career guidance and coaching in understanding call reluctance and applying the counter measures. Thank you one and all.

So up to this point in this text, we've been exploring a sales process, a goal setting process, a street level approach for developing, measuring and responding to metrics and making course corrections based on the metrics. This chapter will tell you why you won't do it! But we have remedies.

Here is a sampling of some of the statements we enjoy making:

"Call reluctance happens only 100% of the time."

"Call reluctance is a natural part of the sales process."

"If you don't think you have call reluctance—don't worry, you do!"

Our (we think) educated view, after working with thousands of sales professionals, is that sales call reluctance is unavoidable. There are sixteen distinct measures of call reluctance. You will have at least one of the sixteen—count on it. One of the greatest challenges in our profession is when we discover a salesperson who has several of the tendencies (high frequency) and/or high severity of certain call reluctance behaviors. We call this (with love) "toxic levels" of call reluctance. These are career-threatening toxic levels of call reluctance.

Stop now and take a quick look at the sales process map on page xvi at the very beginning of this book. Across the top, the first series of checkpoints, we call this "Thinking Great Thoughts"; we set our goals, determined our target accounts, completed our research and verification, and designed our contact strategy. Did you notice that there is no active outbound contacting, just thinking great thoughts?

We have now arrived at the first breakdown in the sales process: failure to execute the contact strategy continuously. The typical cause is call reluctance. Let's drill down to the specifics.

A key reason for even making outbound contact is to promote your products, services and even yourself in an ethical fashion. Call reluctance blocks us from outbound *ethical self-promotion*. Much of this information is available in the text *The Psychology of Sales Call Reluctance: Earning What You're Worth*, authored by George Dudley and Shannon Goodson and published by Behavioral Sciences Research Press.

Hold it right there! What is *ETHICAL* self promotion?

Time for a scenario. Picture this: an instructor-led workshop with 30 sales professionals in attendance. The instructor asks the question, "What do you think of when you hear the term 'Self-Promoter'?" Typical responses:

- Fast talker
- Not team oriented
- Slick, maybe sleazy
- Self interest
- Selfish
- Untrustworthy
- Successful
- Relentless
- Positive
- Caring
- Rich
- Known
- The stereotypical salesman

The responses are pretty much the same, with a variety of positive and negative characteristics. Typically, names of well-known people like celebrities, sports figures, politicians and an occasional business leader come up, and we have an unfair amount of fun with this.

Then the instructor asks another question: "Does anyone know who Sister Nirmala is?"

In over fifteen years of asking this question to thousands of participants, no one knew who Sister Nirmala was. Then the instructor asks a follow-up question:

"Does anyone know of Mother Teresa?"

In over fifteen years of asking this question to thousands of participants, everyone knew who Mother Teresa was.

Well, Sister Nirmala succeeded Mother Teresa as Superior General of the Missionaries of Charity in March 1997.

So, was Mother Teresa a self-promoter? You could imagine the varied reactions of the participants—how could anyone deny that Mother Teresa was a self-promoter? At the very least, she was certainly a promoter for her charity, for her cause. And yet, Sister Nirmala does not seem to be a self-promoter. Hopefully, this helps to break down the barrier of the negative stereotypes of self-promotion.

Now a new question:

Does anyone know who Sister Mary Prema is? You guessed it, successor to Sister Nirmala since March 2009.

There are people who are natural self-promoters, and they possess these three qualities:

1. *Positioning*—they fully utilize their existing contacts, networks and social systems and work to create new ones. A critical aspect of this quality is the *activist* component: "work to create new ones." We suggest that you picture this as a spiral of contacts—an ever-increasing, expanding spiral of contacts. In our world of sales and ethical self-promotion, it can no longer be about a circle of friends or acquaintances; it's about an ever-expanding spiral of contacts.

2. *Style*—what you do that sets you apart from the crowd and gets you remembered. What do you do that gets you remembered? Is it how you respond to a client or prospect? How you dress? Your sense of humor? Your professionalism? Your unique hobby? Your special gift(s)? Pick something. If you can't pick something, that may be what sets you apart and gets you remembered. Could it be your humility?

3. *Consistency*—repeat the process!

And yes, you have to do this consistently.

In summary, our recommendation is to use your ability of self-observation in understanding these three self-promotion qualities. Be mindful of your actions and the actions of others and the effect of ethical self-promotion.

We now move on to the specific call reluctance behaviors, those specific career-threatening blockers of ethical self-promotion. These behaviors produce the lovely effect of reducing your W-2 earnings and limiting the opportunities and options available to you in your life.

We begin with what are inventively called "The Four Impostors." Don't get this wrong—the result of these impostors is exactly the same as the remaining twelve call reluctance behaviors: They downright prevent the necessary volume of outbound contacting. We think you'll find that these really make a lot of sense. You will also note that the remedies are quite different for each of the impostors.

1. *Motivation*

What this is really about is energy level. Do you have the energy available to make the necessary outbound contacts, to "work the room" at a conference, to maintain a regular practice of active prospecting? Without enough physical energy, we're simply not going to make the contact. You know all of the reasons—I'm not feeling well; the baby's been up all night; I'm just beat, etc.

Time for a story. Picture this: an instructor-led workshop for a group of young men in their twenties, in Baltimore, on the Monday morning after Super Bowl Sunday when the Baltimore Ravens won (I'm not making this up—I was there). For the most part, this group of young men were so hung over that their teeth were loose! I made the comment, "You wouldn't be able to make many outbound con-

---

tacts today—you're too hung over." They got the point. Of course, I couldn't get them over the "How about those Ravens, man!"

And what about the remedies for low physical energy? How do we handle that?

- Better sleep
- Exercise
- Better diet
- Coffee
- Red Bull
- Yoga
- Meditation
- Taking breaks
- Proper goal setting
- Contemplating your loved ones
- A vacation
- Your posture: Sit up straight
- Taking care of your body

What can you do today, what action can you take, to help monitor, build, maintain and sustain your energy level?

Time for another story—a personal example.

You should have been there. For ten years, every day at 3:30 in the afternoon, I stopped making outbound contacts. The reason for this is that I knew at that time of day, my prospects were tired. Doesn't that make a lot of sense? My prospects are tired; they don't want to hear from me.

Get this—I'm talking about people I've never met, never spoken to, and I know they're tired. This is psychotic! Well, it's at least delusional. It turns out that *I* was tired at 3:30 in the afternoon, not my prospects!

I never knew this until I took the call reluctance assessment. I thought I was doing a favor for my prospects. And worst of all, after realizing the error of my ways, I did the math and figured out how much this behavior had cost me over the years. I knew my target accounts, the size of those accounts, my hit ratios and my share of the revenue.

Thinking about this another way—as mentioned earlier, I had sixteen appointments a month—now just suppose I was able to arrange two more per month, twenty-four per year, two hundred and forty in ten years. Isn't it true for all of us that if we get in front of two hundred and forty prospects, somebody will buy? Even if we make a mistake, somebody will buy!

I was earning less than I was worth because I was tired at 3:30 in the afternoon. Now that I had recognized this, how did I over-come it? Well, we've instituted guilt-free nap time at Redmond Group—it's in the employee manual. Please don't call us between 2:30 and 3:00p.m. That's a joke—but I do manage to get out of the office, take a walk around the block, maybe have some yogurt—taking care of the body so I can continue working productively on high payoff activities like contacting prospects.

2. Goal Setting, Goal Levels

Earlier in our text we spent a fair amount of time on the mean-ingful, measurable and written characteristics of proper goal setting. Here's an interesting insight. If your goals are out of alignment—for example, too high, too low, not relevant, not written, not clear, not yours, etc.—these characteristics will have a direct negative effect on your energy level.

If goals are set too low, the energy level available to achieve these goals will be low. No inspiration, no excitement about achiev-ing this particular level of success. On the other hand, if your goals are set too high, you experience frustration and burnout combined with the effect of actually reducing your available energy—at least the energy that's available for achievement of your goals. Your energy may increase, however, when you begin to look for another job.

Time for another story:

At one point in my career, I had management responsibility for a fairly large office of a national financial services firm. At that time, we had a network of approximately sixty offices across the country. It was a great job, mostly because of the friendships made with my manager colleagues. One year we were handed our annual revenue goals, which were, in a word, impossible. Quite frankly, there was no relevance to what we had ever accomplished before; the goals were just unreachable. So, in order to keep the morale up with my local team, I explained that in my view, the goals were unreachable, but we should continue to work the best we could, continue to do the smartest things we could, and I would be going back to senior management with a new team goal. I was going to renegotiate these goals. I quickly failed in achieving this goal!

Fast forward about six months, and only 100% of the office managers on my level—sixty of us across the country—had failed to achieve our half-year goals. This was a national team who individually and collectively never thought that we would fail. This just had not occurred to us as a possibility. What happens to people who have good ambition, pretty good smarts and have been used to hitting goals? This is what happened to us: an internal voice says something like, "I'm not going to fail, I'm going to quit." So my colleagues and I began to hint at the fact that we were simultaneously coming up with a new goal—let's quit. Don't get me wrong, this was not some type of conspiracy; this reaction is just natural under the circumstances.

Fortunately, senior management got wind of this and thankfully altered the goals for the second half of the year by making them more realistic. They used what we thought was a pretty good sports analogy: we have the back nine yet to play on the course.

Lesson learned. If you or those you are leading are feeling like quitting (we mean getting a new job and working for one of your competitors), the culprit could be poor goal setting—getting set up to fail. You won't fail, you will quit. You'll be motivated to put your energy and talents to work on getting a new job.

All right, enough on this. What we are really looking for is the ideal combination of high energy that is hard-wired for high goal achievement. Is there anything that might be blocking us from creating and sustaining this high energy, high achievement potential? How can we maintain our energy level? How can we be certain that our goals are truly meaningful, easily measured, and include the features presented in the earlier chapters?

3. Goal diffusion.

You should all be able to easily relate to goal diffusion. The quick description is having too many competing priorities, conflicting goals or just too many things coming at you at once. And this may not simply be because of your employer. It just might be "welcome to your life." Has it become impossible to prioritize? Are *you* in charge of your calendar, for example?

When you experience an unfair share of goal diffusion, the first thing that happens (only one hundred percent of the time) is that your goals drop and become suppressed. You actually become goal avoidant. And—more bad news—this is followed by a drop in your energy level. You burn out (or you will). Other than that, you're fine.

Here's a thought. If your organization has high employee turnover, check to see if goal diffusion could be the culprit. Think about this for yourself. If you are reading this book, it is because you care about yourself and your ability to earn a good living, support your family, etc. You are curious to learn about what may help you in your career, and it never occurs to you that you may fail.

Those are the qualities of the professionals who are actually reading this page—this means you. You're really not thinking about failing —it just doesn't occur to you that that could happen. But with goal diffusion and your goals dropping, followed by lower energy and burnout, you get to a point with your internal dialogue and say something like, "Uh oh, at this rate, I'm going to fail." Followed by, "I'm not going to fail, I'm going to quit!" And then you start dating headhunters. This is a reasonable response to high goal diffusion. You might as well surrender—you cannot sustain high goal diffusion.

We're not talking about temporary goal diffusion; we're all subject to that. A good example is this: Have you ever had the experience of moving your office? What about moving your home? This is what we call temporary goal diffusion. Having to pack, where am I going to be, a new phone system, new address and so on. Check this out with your own experience. The first thing that happens is that outbound contacts drop. I can't make those contacts because I'm too distracted. Where's my stuff, too many other things going on. However, once we're settled in, have the new location set up, know how to use the machines, get our stuff back in order, we can then start making outbound contacts. That's our description and an example of temporary goal diffusion. It happens to all of us. An emergency at home, an emergency with a customer, or whatever it might be. This is typically not the problem.

The goal diffusion we're really concerned about is chronic, long-term goal diffusion. That's what drives goals into a downward spiral, with its companion, burnout, following in close pursuit. How about some suggested remedies?

An exceptionally good remedy is to apply the techniques in Steven Covey's book *First Things First.* We're big fans of Dr. Covey (you might recall his bestseller *The Seven Habits of Highly Effective People*) and have found *First Things First* to be a powerful ally in handling goal diffusion. Covey does not use the term "goal diffusion."

The genius of Covey is that he's asking us if we're working on the big rocks—his analogy for your important, high-payoff activities.

A second key remedy that we coach folks on is calendar management. Notice that we are not using the phrase "time management"—time can't be managed anyway. But calendars can be managed. In Chapter 5, "Appointment Making," we discuss managing the calendar of your prospect. In overcoming goal diffusion, we're driving home the concept of managing your calendar. Here's the technique:

First of all, we really don't care about the type of calendar you are using—electronic or paper. We do care that you use one and only one—have all of your calendar and scheduling information in one place within easy access. Now as for the technique... ready for this? Make an appointment with yourself for purposes of focused outbound prospect contact. Enter/write your name on your calendar; block this time and guard it ferociously. Think of this activity as not in addition to your job—it is a key activity of your job. This appointment with yourself is as important as one with your top client or prospect. Take a quick inventory of the distracting tasks and distracting people that you may be able to eliminate.

Distracting person approaches: "Hi, Tom, do you have a minute?"

Tom responds: "I'm a bit jammed up right now; let's take a look and see when we can meet." (Tom quickly glances at his calendar.) "How about Friday at 5:30? I'm open then."

Distracting person backs away, saying, "On second thought, I think I can handle this myself."

Present moment exercise:

OK, right now, take a look at your calendar for the upcoming week—we *really* mean right now. This is an important exercise that is included in the price you paid for this book. We're not kidding. Go ahead, we'll wait.

Now that you have your calendar ready to go, choose a day and time for focused outbound contact. Here it is: Tuesday from

8:30 to 10:00 a.m. Put your name on your calendar. That's all there is to it.

Let's keep going. Wednesday, 2:00 to 3:15 p.m. Stay with this important theme: "Start from the possible and move to the impossible." You get the idea. And don't stop on Wednesday. While you're at it, take a look at next week and even the following week.

Now for our WARNING! We can pretty much assure you of the following event. OK, your appointment is set and blocked for Wednesday at 2:00 p.m. Here it comes—at about 1:55 p.m. you will want to cancel that appointment! So the discipline of blocking your calendar for the purpose of outbound contact is as important as is execution of the contact strategy.

> Speaking of calendar management, this book would never have been completed without calendar management. And talk about the internal resistance to this! Tom's internal dialogue: "Tom, is this really a high payoff activity? Shouldn't you be using your time better by making more outbound prospecting contacts? And really, who do you think will even read your book? And blah, blah, blah." Oh, hello resistance, my old friend, you just sit over there; I'll pick you up later. Just get the book published—you'll feel better.

One additional suggestion, if you are part of an organization with a sales team in your office, is to block the calendar for the entire team. We've seen this work wonders. Call this your office-wide "Power Hour"—for example, every Thursday, 9:30-10:30 a.m., no other activity except outbound contact for the entire team. No e-mails, no meetings, no administrative reports, no planning, no inward focus on your company—only outbound focus. And we move on to a companywide Power Hour. OK, one more—a worldwide Power Hour: every sales person on the globe making outbound contacts at the same time. And then we move to two Power Hours. Enough?

4. Information

The final impostor is information. Or you can think of it this way: not enough information to effectively prospect. This one is easy to understand and, quite frankly, very easy to overcome. It goes like this: If you don't know what you're talking about, you won't make the outbound contact. If you don't have enough product knowledge, you will be hesitant to contact a prospect.

Think for a moment about the language of your company, your industry, your specialty. We all have a special language connected with our products and services. The obvious solution is to obtain training on your products, and to become a student of your industry through education, earning degrees, participating in networking and social media study groups.

The majority of my career (so far) was in the commercial insurance industry segment as a sales guy. We still do a lot of work in the industry, and when we are reviewing the information and product knowledge call reluctance issues, I remind the participants that at one time, they did not know what BI or PD was. That's bodily injury and property damage. In fact, the entire worldwide multibillion dollar insurance industry is built on only two things that can happen: bodily injury and property damage.

Now in our later years, with more experience, we're really sophisticated in that we have a language. BI can also be referring to business interruption (formerly known as U&O, use and occupancy), we have deductibles and basket deductibles, we have self-insured retentions, offshore and onshore captive insurance companies, alternative risk financing, reinsurance cut through endorsements, long tales, claims made, occurrences, aggregates and basket aggregates, umbrellas, bumbershoots... enough! Got the picture?

WARNING: One of the heads-up we offer here is to make sure you are not working on things or problems that are unsolvable or really don't matter. Do you really need all of that information and product knowledge prior to making contact? Does it matter? So check yourself on this as well. If you find yourself working on problems like these or requesting more product or service information, you may be directly feeding your goal diffusion via over-preparation call reluctance—more on that in the next section. The source of the information, product knowledge and problem solving phenomena can also be your prospect. Has the prospect given you a problem or challenge that is truly unsolvable or even unreasonable? Refer to Chapters 7 and 8 for some suggestions on better qualifying prospective accounts.

CALL RELUCTANCE TYPES

Now we move to the twelve types of call reluctance. I must say that during the initial stages of our call reluctance offering, many of our clients are thinking (some will actually say), "You're making these up." I always urge the audience to keep an open mind and just see if they can relate to any of these characteristics. Please keep in mind, as was stated earlier, that these characteristics, these behaviors are learned. They are NOT character flaws. Criticism and judgment are to be suspended for the next few pages.

Doomsayer

The internal dialogue of a doomsayer goes something like this: "Oh, they'll never be there anyway, why call?"; "They won't like our products"; "We're never going to be able to beat the competitor's price and their spectacular features"; "They probably won't like me and will actually yell at me"; "I'm going to get hung up on"; "It's hopeless." And one actually heard (we hope in jest) at one of our workshops: "Our products and services are mediocre, but at least our prices are high!"

SELLING FROM THE INSIDE OUT

This is the doomsayer. No wonder calls and additional contacts are delayed! How can one stay energized with this relentless internal voice? Expecting the worst and taking few social risks. Hey, this is the voice that kept this book from being completed!

> Time for another story: When I was obtaining the certification of the program from BSRP, we were role playing. I was playing the role of a sales manager and was interviewing a doomsayer sales person. During the session, I came up with what I thought was a brilliant question: "Tell me about the best day you ever had, your best day?" After letting out a sigh, his response was, "Well, I guess that's the day nothing went wrong."

Over-preparation

This is the number-one type of call reluctance your author has. Upon learning that I was an over-preparer, I thought, "What a wonderful quality." That is, until I realized that my activity level was being significantly hampered by my need to over-prepare. An example may help: When I was prospecting for large commercial clients, I would obtain a few years of annual reports, 10K's, and product brochures. We didn't have the web at that time, but if we had, I would have gotten on the web to do more research and fill up my paper and electronic files with useful and needless information and data.

The only problem is that it's then 6:15 p.m. and I haven't made the outbound call. But I'm getting ready! That's what we over-preparers do—we get ready. By the way, another obvious result of over-preparing is that this behavior will directly feed your goal diffusion.

What triggers this? How did I learn this? The trigger is fear: fear that the prospect may ask me a question that I don't know the answer to, and then I'll be found out for the loser I am and live under a bridge and never be able to sell again (no wonder I over-prepare!).

Where did this behavior, this thinking come from? I actually know—from my first boss. If you can, picture this: I was maybe 25 years old, and all I had was a commercial insurance license for the State of New York (that made it legal for me to call on prospects). My boss was a good guy—make that a very good guy—and I was walking out the door to meet with a prospect when my boss said to me, "Tom, have you thought of everything?" And my response was, "I've thought of nothing. His name is Jack, he's on the fifth floor, and he buys insurance, not from us. What else do I need to know?"

Quite frankly, at that time I was really unprepared, and due to the influence of my boss at a very impressionable age, plus the need to keep my job, I immediately adjusted my sales approach and became deeply involved and committed to research. There was an internal need to verify information that was not relevant to simply making an outbound contact. Well, I got so good at this research that a few years later I got promoted. "You're really one of us, Tom." I now had salespeople working for me. So what do you think I was saying to them? "Have you thought of everything? Are you prepared?"

I have to say that for those of you reading this book, if you ever worked with me you're very likely an over-preparer. There are hundreds of salespeople across the country over-preparing because they hung out with me. I'm a carrier of over-preparation call reluctance. I have "toxic" levels of this type of call reluctance, all triggered by what I learned and the positive payoff of this behavior that resulted in promotions and higher earnings. And the trigger of fear that I was taught was that the customer might ask me a question that I don't know the answer to. I might not have the encyclopedic knowledge of every aspect of my product and service. I might not have all the answers, and so on. This is where the fear comes in. How do you like that "I'll live under a bridge" line?

Hyper-Professional

This is a good one, and your author is also a hyper-pro. Observing your own hyper-pro behaviors can be hilarious, so keep your sense of humor engaged. The basic concept is that the hyper-pro works within a mindset that demands an over-investment in image, maintenance and protection of that image, respect, how one might look or sound, and that never-ending discursive internal dialogue of what I think other people may think of me. We're not saying that it's OK to be sloppy or to have little or no investment in how one is viewed. We're describing a "hyper" investment. We've seen entire companies with this phenomenon.

Oh yeah, watch out with hyper-pros where they seek perfection, like having the absolutely perfect proposal supported by the perfect presentation. Once again, these behaviors block us from engaging in outbound, ethical self-promotional activities that can include even getting the proposal out the door.

Some examples may help to clarify. The following are actual statements made by clients. We can't make this up—we're not that clever! Probably there's some tongue-in-cheek in these statements, but you'll get the point:

- Successful sales professional: "I was on my way to a first meeting with a prospect when I noticed that all I had with me was a Bic ballpoint pen. You know the pen; it's the one that's all chewed up on the end. So I stopped at a stationery store, bought a new pen, and it made me late for the meeting. Does that make me a hyper-pro?" Oh, yeah, I think it does. Stuck with maintaining the image that I can't be very good or worthy of your business if I have a pen like this— I'd rather be late for a first meeting!

- Successful sales manager: "I can't visit that prospect; I just had my car washed and there's a dirt road on the way there."

- Here's one for some of the female professionals in the audience. This is an actual statement made by a successful female division manager: "Oh, I have this hyper-pro. If I'm having a bad hair day, I will not call a prospect—what if they want to see me right away?" Incidentally, when I give these examples in our classes, the women in the audience usually respond with something like "I can understand that bad hair idea, but that pen story is just stupid!"

- Successful sales professional: "I'm sitting in a Starbucks in New York City ready to go into a prospect meeting and I'm thinking, 'If I spill coffee on myself, I'll cancel the meeting and go shopping.' " The real message here is that I would ruin my image by showing up with coffee on my dazzling white shirt and crisply ironed slacks, shined shoes and new sports jacket. At least I have a couple of spare ties in my briefcase!

Stage Fright

It's a safe bet that we all know what stage fright is. One of my most successful sales professionals had toxic levels of stage fright. I worked with Bill for years, carried his briefcase for him and never knew about his stage fright. How would I know? I found out upon his taking the SPQ*GOLD assessment. I said, "Stage fright— What's that about?" Bill responded, "I've spent my entire career not getting up in front of groups." He had adjusted his career and product knowledge by becoming a leading international specialist in a unique complex financial instrument where one-on-one selling was the most effective means of delivering the intended solutions to a client.

The tragedy here is that he was my best salesman, who was producing around a million dollars of new revenue annually, but perhaps he could have produced two million. If I had known about his stage fright, I could have put people and resources around him as support. The stage fright is sometimes so hidden that it can actually work in a sequence like this:

1. He wouldn't make an outbound contact because
2. He might get an appointment that
3. Could lead to a qualified opportunity that
4. Could lead to a proposal and
5. The proposal might have to be presented to a group.

So, due to the fact that there was a possibility that he might have to get up in front of a group, the outbound contacts were never started. This is one of those regrets I have in my career—being blind to this behavior in my best guy.

Our work with stage fright brought to light another interesting insight. Stage fright can exist even when working with small groups like four or five people. It really has to do with the way we exchange energy. For example, people who have a high degree of stage fright are typically thinking about the terror associated with making a presentation or speech in front of large audiences. On the other hand, working with small groups like four people might actually energize them. However, go work in front of a group of four hundred people, and they pass out.

The reason for this is that, in a small group, you absorb the energy of the group, and in a large group you give out your energy. In my case, my experience is exactly the opposite. When working with a small group, I give my energy away, and at the end of the session, I'm exhausted. With four hundred or four thousand in the audience, I rock the house because I absorb energy under those conditions. This is a way to assure all of us that there is no criticism about having stage fright; it is simply the way we exchange energy.

The good news is that there is at least one wonderful remedy: take a look at Toastmasters International. They know how to overcome stage fright, how to improve your delivery—they got it right. Expect phenomenal results.

Role Rejection

Does anyone remember Herb? Herbert Ruggles Tarlek, Jr., the boorish, tasteless advertising sales executive who wears loud plaid suit jackets and striped pants, with his belt matching his white shoes, at WKRP in Cincinnati? If you can remember Herb (or even picture him), you now know about Role Rejection: "I don't want to be one of those slick, sleazy salespeople like Herb Tarlek." This is the stereotype of the salesperson that we all know—certainly not our salesperson hero. Another interesting phenomenon in the United States, and we suspect around the world, is that in the last seventy or so years of filmmaking, anytime a salesperson has been depicted, it has been with a hugely negative spin. The stereotype is constantly reinforced and actually built into our culture.

How many of our readers have the word "Sales" on their business cards? Or are you a "Regional Client Relationship Manager" or a "Business Initiator" or an "Account Executive" or "Client Advocate"? Please—anything but sales!

We experience role rejection in all sorts of ways:

- During telephone calls: "This is not a sales call."

- At face-to-face new business appointments: "I'm not here to sell you anything."

- And how about at company internal sales meetings: "You never want to be too sales(y) with prospects."

- On our business cards

One of the observations we've made over the years has to do with an ability to create and maintain energy, interest, enthusiasm, etc. for what you do on a day-to-day basis. If you cannot sustain the energy required to be successful, you will fail (but at least you'll be miserable every day!). It's quite interesting to us that those who abhor the thought of being in sales (role rejection) are naturally NOT in sales and never will be!

An example may be helpful. When we review a call reluctance assessment with an individual who is not in a sales role, the results typically indicate that there is a frequency and severity of various types of call reluctance behaviors. And role rejection can be on the top of the list. Our conversation usually goes something like this: "Congratulations, you're in exactly the right job." This statement really relaxes the person, and a window opens through which we can have a meaningful discussion and coaching session.

The reason the person is not in sales is that he or she cannot sustain the energy needed to be successful in that role. And yet, he likes to eat regularly, live indoors and support his family—so he gravitated to a work situation where he can create and sustain energy. Good for him! Think about this for yourself: While it's a pretty good bet that there are parts of your job that you would really rather not have to do, you do them because the "package" of the job is acceptable. There are parts of the sales process that I would rather not have to do, but they must be done. If there was a way around them, believe me, we would have found it by now.

Yielder

The internal dialogue of a Yielder goes something like this:

- "I don't want to bother them today."

- "It's Monday, the prospect won't want to hear from me today, they just got back from their weekend."

- "I don't want to bother them today, it's Friday."

- "It's too close to lunch. I'm not going to call now."

- "It's just after lunch; they just got back and have calls to return."

- "It's summer. I'll get to them right after Labor Day."

- "There's a holiday weekend coming up."

Can you see a pattern here? Have you said or thought these same things? Have you heard your colleagues use the same dialogue? How about from your boss or your sales manager?

Yielder is the number one type of call reluctance in the United States. We are a nation of yielders. But doesn't it feel right? Doesn't it seem to make sense? Doesn't it feel like we're describing a terrific quality that we can aspire to?

The key characteristic of a yielder is that he does not want to be perceived as being pushy or intrusive. We see this in behaviors like not asking for the order, not asking for a referral, not asking for additional needed information, etc. In our work with yielders over the years we've discovered two additional characteristics; one is a quality, and the other can have a negative effect on self-promoting activities.

We'll start with the negative. The yielder can have the tendency to put the needs of others in front of his own. That sounds like a terrific quality, except that the yielder does it to a fault. By putting the needs of others in front of your own, you can directly feed your own goal diffusion. The yielder winds up carrying other people—your co-workers, your boss, customers, suppliers, distributors, family members, those on the committee with you at church, Little League, PTA, etc. The yielder has a very difficult time saying "no." He can take on way too many obligations of others.

Another quality of a yielder (and this is a good one) is that the yielder has an uncanny ability to develop strong relationships. In our view, he does not even know how he is doing it. We think it has to do with his ability to listen, to empathize and to relate to others as human beings, particularly during one-on-one interactions. This is a wonderfully positive quality of a yielder. This is where we counsel these folks to "Exploit that quality!" Of course, the yielder has a difficult time "exploiting" anything (even his own terrific qualities), which is probably another reason why he is so adept at creating strong relationships.

A personal example: Why is it that when I'm working with a room full of salespeople for a few hours that with any yielders in the room, I feel like I've known them for years? It amazes me. Ten hours of instructor-led facilitation over a few days, and with yielders it's equal to about a four-year relationship. Exploit that quality!

Social Self-Consciousness

Notice how we're beginning our descriptions of each of these call reluctance tendencies with an active internal dialogue that goes something like this:

"I don't want to call on that person because he/she has..."

- more money

- more power

- more prestige

- a better title

- higher education level

- a vacation home

- a Porsche 944 Turbo in the driveway

- he's taller (you can't make this up).

We've also heard it said: "I won't call on him/her because he's a man/she's a woman."

The most extreme case I have ever come across was in a room full of certified financial planners. One of the gentlemen admitted, "Oh, yes, I have this social self-consciousness call reluctance. I won't contact anyone who has more than fifteen million in assets." I was a bit shocked and offered an immediate (but not too helpful) response: "Are there a lot of them in this neighborhood? You'll be fine with the twelve's!" It was fascinating to me that this upper limit was somehow put into his mind. Once the prospect reached fifteen million or above, he or she became untouchable. So where did that come from? This is another great example of the fact that these thoughts, this internal discourse, is taught to us.

Briefly speaking, social self-consciousness call reluctance will block us from interacting with the "up market"—which reminds me of another short story. One of our new sales people said to me (thankfully in a private conversation) that she was uncomfortable calling on rich, successful people. So I suggested that she call on only poor, unsuccessful people. This is a good example of a word-based remedy, and wow, did it work well. I saw the transition right in front of me. She got it.

Separationist

This is an interesting tendency: hesitancy to call on friends for purposes of self-promotion. This one is very common and, in our experience, can be quite severe. The individual with separationist call reluctance will typically preach it from the mountaintop: "Do not call on your friends, ever!!"

We like to offer an easy response for this one. "Call on those who are not your friends—you have an unlimited supply! You can't get to them all!" Words of caution, however: Watch out when you become friends with your client or prospect or referral source and then you stop making contact with them. This has happened to me —I've stopped interacting with clients and even prospects who became friends.

Emotionally Unemancipated

OK, so you won't call on family. See the separationist comments. Call on those who are not your family—you have an unlimited supply. And you will run out of prospects pretty quickly if you're only going to work on your family.

Referral Aversion

Some of the internal dialogue that we've heard:

- "Oh, it's not time yet to ask for a referral."

- "I don't want to be beholden to anyone."

- "I don't want to seem too greedy or too needy."

- "What if they say no?"

- "What if they give me the wrong type of referral?"

- "I asked for a referral once in 1978—it didn't go well and probably won't go well now."*

- "Asking for referrals—isn't that a bit like asking someone for help? I'd rather go it alone."

Referral sources are terrific. Referrals are magical. Referrals represent the fastest way to get business in the door. When working for referrals, you really become a sales manager who is managing your referral sources. Congratulations—you're no longer in the sales business, you're in the sales management business!

Some national statistics may help in driving us to harvest referrals:

1. Over 90% of those asked would offer referrals.

2. Only 3% of the available referral sources are actually asked.

3. Your closing ratio starts at 50% and goes *up* from there!

*Incidentally, this is one of those call reluctance characteristics that will be reinforced and re-lived every time you are thinking about asking for a referral. If it didn't go well in 1978, the same chemical reaction in your body will take place today.

Telephobia

...is defined as hesitancy to use the phone for outbound contact. We are still big advocates of using the phone as a tool for conducting outbound self-promotional activities. We're NOT talking about returning a call, responding to an inquiry, fulfilling client service responsibilities and all the normal routines of our day-to-day work. We're talking about self-directed, disciplined use of the phone for outbound contacts.

OK, we know you've been waiting for them, so here are some of the voices we hear:

- "I'd rather drive across town to see if they're in than to pick up the phone and call them" (we're not making this up—actual discussion with a salesperson).

- "I don't want to be one of those tele-salespeople that call us at dinner."

- "It's totally ineffective; I'd rather use e-mail, fax, FedEx, UPS, USPS and/or telepathy." We've said this before: our next book should be *Sales by Telepathy: Never Having to Make Another Outbound Contact* (that really does sound like a good book!).

It is so interesting to us that we can walk into a company and tell within the first few minutes if telephobia is alive and well. Just take a look at the owners or leaders. If the phone in the owner's office is on the credenza behind her and there are three days of the *Wall Street Journal* piled on top of the phone, we know there is telephobia in the operation. On the other hand, if the owner is walking around the enterprise with a hands-free wireless headset, we know there is little, if any, telephobia here.

This tells you another thing about the culture—are the employees relying on their internal voicemail to answer the phones, or are they diving for the phone as it rings? The diving part will separate you from your competitors. It is a strategic competitive advantage if you answer the phone and actually return phone calls (but I digress). The good news about telephobia in our view is that it is the easiest call reluctance tendency to get over.

And we've saved the most difficult for last:

Oppositional Reflex

This describes the person who is ultimately not teachable or coachable, but at least they are closed-minded! In the behavioral sciences parlance, these good people are the workshop leader's nightmare. We've been there, and you know these people as well—arms crossed, heels jammed into the carpet with that "show me" expression across their furrowed brows. They basically put a considerable amount of energy into critiquing and complaining rather than promoting. Keep in mind that *this behavior is a reflex—it bypasses the person's thinker.* There is a terrific write-up on this topic in the text *The Psychology of Sales Call Reluctance: Earning What You're Worth.* You may particularly like the section "I am not oppositional, you S.O.B.!"

We have a few memorable stories on this, and here's one. Picture this: a workshop series to be conducted over a ten-week period in which we alternated workshops and conference calls every other week. There were fourteen people in the program, but at least (only) twelve were toxic oppositionals! We knew this because we had their completed assessment results beforehand. We dubbed this our Welcome to Hell Sales Series.

Our first three-hour workshop went as expected: arms crossed, heels dug into the carpet, etc. Even the customer who had ordered the program was against us. Due to our ability and considerable talent at displaying heartfelt charm and engendered endearment (along with a good dose of compassion for these folks), by the conclusion of the first half-day instructor-led session, we had made some good progress and developed reasonable relationships with the team.

Upon our return two weeks later, you would have thought we had never been there. In the intervening two weeks, the program had been undermined. By the mid-point of the second classroom session, I went to the manager and told her, "They aren't having fun and neither are we, so we're resigning from the assignment." Well, guess what? They opposed that as well! Please don't leave— oh no, we're out of here. Best wishes are flying your way.

Incidentally, we are happy to inform our readers that although oppositional reflex exists, the condition is rather rare in business. We can only conclude that if the enterprise had oppositionals on board, it is likely they sent them to competitors to oppose them!

Remedies for Overcoming Sales Call Reluctance

Now a bit about the remedies. I must admit that when George Dudley introduced the countermeasures, I was very skeptical. So skeptical, in fact, that during my initial certification process, I spoke to George and told him that I could not continue. I literally could not see myself at some future time, standing up in front of a room full of professional adults and talking about the psychological hocus pocus that George was describing. George said something like, "Tom, put your skepticism on the side; you can pick it up later on your way out… and besides, I don't give refunds!" I'm happy to report that I followed through with George's suggestion and found the remedies to be not only fascinating, but effective—they work.

Before we go further here, we could never do justice to the intensive explanations for each of the six main types of remedies. For an in-depth presentation, please refer to *The Psychology of Sales Call Reluctance* text. Basically there are two types of countermeasures: Mechanical and Word-Based.

The Mechanical Procedures are not dependent on words, are based on brain wiring, agreement is not necessary, and understanding is not necessary. In other words—Just do it! My own interpretation of the mechanical procedures is that they bring my mind and body back to the present moment. Here's how it works. I'm sitting at my desk and not making outbound contacts because of (for example) my over-preparation tendencies. My body is happily sitting here not making calls, just experiencing the sights and sounds of the office or the environment, the weight of my body on the chair, my feet on the floor, etc.

But my mind is a world away: that internal dialogue again of a possible future conversation with a prospect and possibly being asked a question I don't know the answer to and (enough—please refer to the over-preparation section in this chapter so I can stop over-preparing!) So the bottom line is that my body is not connected with my mind; the emotion of fear is triggered by the expectation that something will go wrong in the future. When the mechanical procedures are used, the result is that my mind and body are now in the present moment, and there is very little fear in the present moment!

These procedures work in golf as well. In fact, they work in most sporting events. Ever see a particular motion or what seems to be an unusual habit of a professional player—like a batter touching his cap, a basketball player with a wrist band, or a tennis player who bounces the ball a set number of times before each serve? These are mechanical procedures to bring one to the present moment. That last missed shot is history; let's get on the next one quickly and efficiently.

To spark your interest, here is a short description of the three types of mechanical procedures (put your skepticism off to the side; you can pick it up later after you finish reading).

1) Thought Zapping
   - One of the most powerful techniques available.

- Disconnects a recalled experience from its associated unpleasant feelings.
- Provides the opportunity to replace negative images with positive ones.

2) Threat Desensitization
- Reduces the effect of fear.
- Best suited for very specific call reluctance fears.
- Fears are identified, organized and de-stigmatized one at a time.

3) Sensory Injection
- Can be used with any of the five senses.
- Solicits positive sensations while in an anxiety provoking situation.
- Can be used both for relaxation and self-confidence.

The Word Based Procedures are based on self persuasion. Agreement is necessary and understanding is necessary. The explanations below should help. There are three types of Word Based Remedies/Procedures:

1) Thought Realignment (We're back to self-talk.)
- Based on the belief that most of our distressful feelings are caused by the *view we take* of things and situations in life, not the things and situations themselves.
- Works best to prevent call reluctance.

Here's a kind of poem we picked up from Behavioral Sciences Research Press:

> "What you say
> Influences what you feel
> And alters what you do
> If you want to change what you do
> Modify what you feel
> By altering what you say."

So, if you wake up every morning and your opening line of the day is "I wonder what is going to go wrong today?" ...Guess what?

Here's an example of thought realignment in action. I have two daughters who are out in the world and launched. But I have a picture of them on my desk of when they were small. I look at this picture and I can hear their voices saying, "Dad, we're relying on you to make the next call." I'm persuaded, I agree and understand this statement—my thoughts of not making outbound calls are realigned.

2) Fear Inversion
   - Although it is quite fascinating, it cannot be described.
   - It must be followed, step by step, as outlined in the book.

3) Negative Image Projection
   - This is based on the understanding that self-limiting habits become strengthened and ingrained by repetition. For example, "I asked for a referral in 1978, and it didn't go well." So every time you are about to ask for a referral, the identical feelings arise.

Almost the final word: I'm not the source of the scientific process nor the exceptional scientific approach behind this work— just a sales guy. But I do know this. This assessment and the BSRP professionals supporting this work dramatically transformed the way I was conducting business. It transformed my sales team when I had a traditional, high-paying, prestigious job, and since then has transformed thousands of other sales professionals we've had the privilege of working with. As mentioned earlier, we have a deep gratitude to George Dudley and Shannon Goodson for discovering these phenomena and devoting their professional lives to this practice. For more information, please feel free to contact BSRP. If you're hesitant to do that, you may be experiencing call reluctance. OK then, call a prospect instead.

(Your Name), Inc. Sales Process

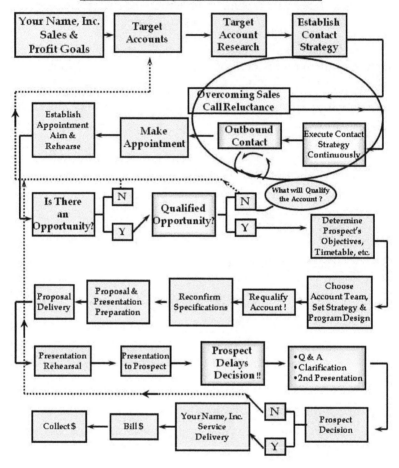

Copyright ©Redmond Group, Inc. 2011

Chapter 5

APPOINTMENT MAKING
Now to the Street

In Chapters 2 and 3 we developed targeting and contact strategies. The development process started by taking the widest, most inclusive perspective on our characteristics as account-targeters, and on the characteristics of the targets themselves. We then tried to see if we could tilt the "numbers game" a little in our favor by taking the time to look for opportunities to move some of the cold targets to the "warm" end of the range. Warm targets are higher hit-ratio opportunities than cold targets. In following this path we have, as a by-product, started to build a reservoir of information about ourselves, our firms, and our prospects that grows (quickly) and is available to us on an ongoing basis, empowering and injecting confidence into all of our business development activity.

This strategy falls naturally into place from an overarching principle of the Sales Process Map—a web of relationships is our basic working unit. The web is the basic unit for our *goals* (a web of the personal and the professional). It's the essence of *ourselves as prospectors* (a "self" that extends back through all of our experiences and acquaintances, and forward to our goals. A "self" that's additionally extended through our *firm's* past, present and future). It's the place where we meet our *prospects* (through their web of relationships—past, present and future).

Maybe we've warmed up a couple of prospects. But the majority are still cold. And they're worthy targets. So how do we get in front of them and build relationships? It's time to go out the door (or at least for our *voices* to go out the door) and get some appointments. What's our first stop as we head out? That's right! Our goals.

Let's flip back to Chapter 1 and go to the tracking instructions at the end of the chapter. Recall how you figured out how many new business meetings you needed to have per month in order to maintain the level of active, "proposed" business that will take you to your income goal. The income goal is telling you the number of appointments you have to make.

Before we hit the phones, let's get a clear sight on the number of calls we need to make in order to end up with the right number of appointments. This requires an easy bit of data mining. Do you know how many calls it takes you, on average, to get one meeting? No? Then look back through your prospect management system and figure it out. You don't maintain a prospect management system? We're getting more valuable by the sentence! From now on, you're going keep a written (or word-processed) record of your calling activities. That's the good news. The better news is that you've just committed to a vital instrument for building your way to your income goal.

We're not interested in promoting any particular program. Microsoft Outlook works fine, and it's probably already installed on your computer. There are plenty of other sales assistance programs and, as far as we're concerned, legal paper and #2 pencil could work if you are organized enough to develop a useful system. We're all for substance over form. At a minimum, we're interested in keeping track of:

- the overall number of calls made for a given time segment (day, week, month)

- a history of activity on each call ("scheduled meeting for Tuesday, April 1, 10:00 am" or "left voicemail re: scheduling phone app't. for Tuesday, April 8, 10:00 am")

- scheduled follow-ups

It doesn't take a lot of sophisticated software to generate some useful information, and the call-to-meeting hit rate is *very* useful.

We've discovered at Redmond Group that our call-to-meeting ratio is about ten to one. We make ten phone calls in order to schedule one appointment with a targeted prospect. We take that information right from recorded notes in our prospect management system. So, if we have figured out (with the tracker) that we need sixteen meetings each month in order to generate enough active proposals to set us on the path to our income goals, then we have to make one hundred and sixty calls to get there. One hundred and sixty calls!

Getting a Grip

Is one hundred and sixty calls a mind-bendingly awesome undertaking, or is it, as they said on the streets in the Bronx of my youth, "Nuttin' "? Believe it or not, it's a lot closer to "nuttin' " than it is to scaling Mount Everest. Did you just say, "Prove it to me"? OK, we'll provide the backup.

You may have developed the impression that we have a tendency to quantify things here at the "Sense of Humor" headquarters. It could then be said that you've arrived at an accurate assessment of our belief in the utility of quantification, entitling you to continue reading.

We've measured how long it takes, on average, to dial a number, wait through the ring, wait through the recorded greeting (be it friendly or "pit bullish" in tone), leave a quality message, and hang up. It takes about one minute and fifty seconds. There's a reason we picked "leaving a voice-mail message" as the standard call measure. (Here comes another number!) It's the way that eighty-six percent of your dials are going to go. They'll be picked up by voice-mail. No kidding. We'll discuss the art of leaving an effective voice-mail message in short order.

What are these numbers telling us? They're telling us that it takes five hours to hit your targeted number of calls. Assuming you're a nine-to-fiver (if you're reading this book, you're not), and that you take an hour out of the office for lunch (an hour—how quaint!) and your three o'clock walk (which you probably don't take but should), then you have one hundred and sixty hours to wedge that five hours of calling into per month. Notwithstanding the fact that there are internal sales and management meetings, appointments with customers, thinking great thoughts, fire drills, calls from the spouse, calls from the children, calls from the baby sitter, calls from the boyfriend, power shortages, sick days, snow days, alien invasions, etc., your "must do," value-enhancing call time amounts to about three percent of a month in the workplace. Numbers can help us put things in perspective. One hundred and sixty calls isn't scaling Mount Everest. It's more like climbing a small stepladder.

There's also plenty of time to do the research on targets that might uncover some information and help elevate your call from the "Hi, how ya doin'?" variety. Let's not forget, each call is like a chance in the batter's box. You don't want to squander it. The fact that most calls go to voicemail in no way diminishes the care with which they are handled. Consistency and professionalism are the best wrappers for your increasing value, and the value you present to prospects.

Our ten-calls-per-meeting average is spread over a range of frequencies. We've found that a referral produces a "one call, one meeting" ratio, or pretty darn close to it. On the other hand, if we're calling a cold, very large prospect, a different pattern has emerged: Seven calls to get to the wrong person, but someone who can, finally, point you to the end of the trail. We're talking about the "average" number of calls per meeting. That means that we count each call until we get to the right party, whether it takes two or ten calls. It all comes out in the numbers.

Unburden Thyself

We've put some perspective on the magnitude of the goal-driven, appointment-getting portion of our value-enhancement process (no hyphens in the next sentence, I promise). It's not overwhelming. In fact, it's perfectly sized for success.

There's another topic we want to highlight, another way to clear the path for maximum efficiency in nailing down meetings. We've noticed over the years that two questions often arise in connection with the mechanics of calling for appointments. They head the list of major preoccupations of our clients. The questions are

1) "When is the best time to make calls?"
and
2) "How often should you call prospects?"

The answers are:

1) "When you're conscious."
and
2) "Until they surrender."

In other words, unburden yourself of these questions. They cause a simple procedure to become weighted down with unnecessary baggage. Beware of overtaxing the process by trying to conjure up answers to concerns that don't merit the trouble. At Redmond Group, we've encountered an infinity of hard-wired rules of thumb from clients, like "don't call on Fridays or Mondays" or "don't call just before or just after holidays" or "only call before 9:00 am or after 5:30 pm." We've heard, "She was so nice and receptive when we first spoke. But now she never returns my voicemails. And she *encouraged* me to follow up. She's irritated with me. And I'm irritated with *her*. I think I'll drop her off my list, after I send an indignant e-mail."

If these rules of thumb *ever* had validity, they lost it over four decades ago when the solicited became overwhelmed by hordes of salespeople who all miraculously discovered the *same* perfect times to call. And no prospect is going to miss you and go searching for you if you suddenly drop off the map in a huff. We're not looking for ways to *reduce* our precious allotment of time. The chances of our being able to *intuit* the right moment to call are close to zero. Now there's a coincidence for you: the exact same success rate produced by telepathizing for new business.

All of the mental wrangling that goes into the hocus pocus of "*Now* she's going to pick up and take my call!" or "Tomorrow feels right for her!" creates a big drain on your increasingly valuable energy reserves. We want to be as nimble as possible. We travel light. We don't want to shackle ourselves by spending thought on picking that perfect set of circumstances for calling. It's always the right time to call. Unless, of course, you're unconscious. It's that simple. And don't forget that eighty-six percent of your calls are going to be answered by voicemail, and there *really* isn't a best time.

The point is that, perhaps counter-intuitively, you have to take yourself out of the picture when it comes to making calls. It's both easy *and* debilitating to allow self-induced angst to develop in this arena. If you bring too much analysis (perhaps *any* analysis, beyond on which side of your head to place the receiver) to this part of the process, then you're stealing from the reservoir of energy you've built with your personal and professional goals. Calling is a "clean room" operation—no contaminants. It's a scalpel, not a Greek drama.

How about calling "until they surrender"? Isn't that a little more clever than it is realistic? No. Again, it goes to the point of getting out of your own head and giving up on the idea of getting into your prospect's head before they're even a client.

When asked how we built our firm to a referral basis, we've sometimes responded, "We called ten thousand prospects and some of them bought." That's not just a glib dodge. It's a fact. The Sales Process Map is forged on the smithy anvil of experience. When I left the 10,000- plus-employee brokerage firm to form Redmond Group, I took with me a list of everyone I knew and had ever known in the insurance world. I pounded that list hard to get my first piece of business. The list produced exactly zero clients.

Why? The people I already knew weren't buyers of what I was selling. They might have been powerfully placed good buddies, but they weren't within my target. I had to find that out. I had faith that I had something valuable to offer, but I had to turn that faith into food, mortgage payments and college tuition. My old rolodex wasn't working out. What was left was the great unknown, the world of cold prospects. We targeted different business categories and hammered away. We ran down some dead ends, but over time, we arrived at where we are now, picking through opportunities that come to *us*.

There's a certain characteristic that might result from a genetic mutation, but I believe it has something to do with our success. I take *nothing* personally with a prospect. When they become a paying customer, then I'm emotionally invested, because then they're part of my personal and professional mosaic, and I'm part of theirs. Until that time we both know absolutely nothing about whether or how one might bring benefit to the other.

I call people. I have something valuable to offer them. The value of my service doesn't deteriorate over time. Why should my support for it deteriorate?

My list of contacts from the insurance business? It has value even though it never produced a direct deal. Remember the part (Chapter 2) about getting to know yourself as a targeting instrument? There's a world of information-gathering potential and referral possibilities on that list, and a world of opportunity for me to be of assistance to old friends.

As you develop the habit of paying attention to the mundane routines of everyday life (inside and outside of business), interesting, useful and quantifiable patterns emerge. And we've got one right here! We've noticed that we must have fifty percent of our quota for monthly meetings booked by the first day of the month or we won't hit the mark. Why is that interesting? Because it's another guidepost that lets us verify that we're on the path to our year-end income goal. It shows us whether or not an adjustment should be made—for example, making more calls or modifying our target selection.

A Few Worthy Generalizations About Calling

We're now going to be taking a look at "on the ground" settings through which we encounter prospects on the telephone. Calling for appointments is where the sales process most often breaks down. How often? About one hundred percent of the time.

We've set the background for booking appointments by quantifying the number of calls and the hourly allocation we need to apply in order to achieve our income goals. And remember, only small items are actionable. We've seen how each individual call is a small unit and that these units add up to a very manageable aggregate.

We've also dipped into a little psychology. Experience has shown us that there's a tendency to bring too much "self" to the calling process. We want to travel light and leave our psycho-histories at the door when we're calling prospects. Each individual call is simply a small probe that might turn into an opportunity for you to be of service to someone and, as a natural consequence, to supply energy to your reservoir of personal and professional goals.

Worthy generalizations:

- Purpose: The call is for one purpose and one purpose only —to get a meeting. You're not on the phone to sell, or to make a friend. It's too early for that kind of stuff. *Everything* —what you say, how you say it, whether it's a voicemail message, a message left with an assistant, a direct conversation with your prospect, no matter *what*—it's all about getting a meeting. Singleness of purpose is our mantra.

- Professionalism: Again, whether it's voicemail or direct conversation, your tone and content must be crisp and professional. You are valuable and your prospect is valuable. The links between you must *always* be equal to the important cargo they carry.

We'll spend some time taking a look at where our dials are going to end up: on voicemail, in the hands of a gatekeeper (an assistant or co-worker), or in direct conversation with our targeted prospect. How do we strategize toward landing a meeting? Let's see.

Voicemail

We noted earlier that eighty-six percent of your calls are going to be picked up by voicemail. That's the fact in today's business world. Our experience shows us that the best, highest-reward approach to this state of affairs is to stick with the concepts that have been mentioned already:

- figure out the number of calls you have to make in order to hit your appointment requirement

- make the calls

- don't spend energy trying to figure out when or how many times to call

- remember that the only purpose of the call is to get an appointment

- *always* maintain a professional demeanor.

The overriding principle is that voicemail is here to stay, and we've got to get rid of any lingering feelings we may hold that it's an annoyance or an obstacle. It's neither. It's simply a fixture of the territory we're navigating on our way to goal fulfillment. *Every* interface with a prospect, including voicemail, is important and bears our imprint.

Some recommendations:

- Always leave a voicemail. Get out of the "to leave or not to leave" debate. Don't assume that the prospect's gotten tired of your voice and hits "delete" before you've reached the end of the first syllable. Maybe she does. But *you* don't know that, and it doesn't advantage you in any way to make that assumption. In fact, it diminishes the effectiveness of your message if you allow that debate to occur, even in your mental background.

- Begin your message with solid, confidently-delivered items, things you actually know: your name, your company, the date and time. The prospect is interested in goods and services that will benefit her in the fulfillment of her responsibilities. *Very* briefly state the purpose of your call. Perhaps you've researched and identified a niche or new product that the prospect's developing. Say that, and state that your firm's a leader in providing relevant services to firms with similar backgrounds. You'd like to find an open spot on her calendar to share your experience and insights and determine if they bear beneficially on her circumstances. Good-bye. (Don't meander.)

- Leave your phone number. Twice. Spoken slowly. Professionally. No jokes.

Q. If the overwhelming percentage of calls are going to end up on voicemail, then isn't this process—day-in, day-out—a mind-numbing, useless waste of time?

A. No. But we forgot to mention that nobody's going to call you back. Ever. And if someone *does* call you back, it's a warning that they're probably desperate for someone to pull them out of some sort of fire.

One of the great salvations and sustaining magic principles for all of us is that THINGS CHANGE. I remember making forty-four calls to a prospect and having a colleague say, "Why are you doing that? It looks like a waste of time." But I knew two things:

1) It was actually very little time, less than an hour and twenty minutes over the eighteen months.

2) It doesn't benefit me to decide unilaterally that it's time to stop.

3) Things change.

Sure enough, I called one day and the guy was gone. I had an appointment with his replacement after two more calls. On average, things are going to open up for you. That's how it works. I don't know *why* it works; that's not my department. I just know *that* it works. I know that I get almost all of my business from referrals, and I started out doing just what I'm outlining here. One day the prospect's going to pick up. When that happens I've sometimes said, "Could you please put me through to your voicemail? I've forgotten how to speak with humans." (OK, I allow myself the occasional joke.)

The point is, every call's an important call, and you and your prospect deserve professionalism, voicemail or not. Every message you leave, answered or not, is an opportunity to reinforce your image. The people on the other end know what you're up against; they've experienced voicemail stonewalling. X % of them will eventually want to see you just to make sure that the dogged voice really belongs to a body.

Gatekeeper

Sometimes your call will be answered by the assistant to your targeted prospect. This person's a vanishing breed. Perhaps they're not really vanishing, they just don't answer a boss's phone as often as they used to, or type letters for others. They might be administrative assistants for a group of people. The gatekeeper is a wily but potentially very helpful person. She's used to the fact that every salesperson thinks that he or she can cajole her into setting up a meeting. She's an ace at yessing people to death while keeping the door firmly shut, and she hates patronizing smoothies.

Gatekeepers are to be dealt with at the same level of professionalism that applies to direct conversation with the targeted prospect. We'll talk about phone dialogue when we get to direct conversation. Our purpose here is to get a meeting with the prospect.

You should identify yourself and your firm to the gatekeeper and briefly state the purpose of your call (to set up an appointment with the prospect). No selling. Make sure you get the assistant's name, title, direct line, and e-mail address. Then listen. You're not the first salesperson she's heard from, and you're not going to convert her to lobbying on your behalf with the first call. Listen to what she says, get any clarifications you need, and get off the phone.

It takes time to develop a relationship with a gatekeeper. They have important responsibilities and will have to be convinced that you bring something valuable to the table before they'll recommend that the prospect should meet you. By listening, you might learn about her firm's and the prospect's concerns as they apply to your services. Take your time. She *might* be able to help you, but she can *certainly* crush you.

It can also be useful, once you've left a few voicemails with the prospect, to determine if the prospect does, in fact, work in conjunction with a proactive assistant. You must tread carefully along this path of "assistant relations." Developing a relationship with a gatekeeper can lead to very useful information about "goings on" within the targeted company, and perhaps can open the door to an appointment with the targeted prospect.

We advise, however, that it's possible to get "side-tracked" by a gatekeeper and shuttled off to the freight yard of "derelict solicitors." Keep all of your options open. Don't invest one hundred percent in the idea that the gatekeeper is going to perform magic for you and open the door to success. There's great seductive power in having a warm voice to speak with instead of a cold machine.

Make no assumptions. Get out of the crystal-ball game. You have no way of interpreting the relationship between the gatekeeper and the prospect until you learn it from the *prospect*. Until such time, keep leaving your regularly scheduled voicemails with the prospect while maintaining your relationship with the gatekeeper. And stay detached. Beyond an appropriately friendly professional demeanor, don't hang any greater emotional expectation on a gatekeeper than you would on a voicemail machine. After the firm becomes a paying client, you can take them *both* out to dinner.

Direct Conversation

The purpose of a one-on-one conversation with a prospect is to get an appointment. No matter what direction the conversation takes, it's your job to bring it back to a scheduled meeting. The "fill" for every gap in a conversation is, "How's next Thursday? Nine o'clock works for me." There's no exaggerating this point.

You're not on the phone to make small talk (heaven forbid!). You are a professional with goal-oriented responsibilities, and you're talking with a professional with her own set of responsibilities. Don't ask her how she's doin'. You're not there yet. You're a voice that may or may not be carrying useful information. Starting off with a probe into the prospect's physical or psychological well-being is a flat-footed momentum-killer. And it lumps you together with all of the other anxious aspirants. Get to the point in a deliberate, professional manner:

- your name (don't remind her that you've left eight voicemails; it doesn't matter now)

- your firm's name

- the purpose of your call (you've learned something about the prospect's business and you're an expert in providing applicable solutions or products in relevant situations)

- you want to see if she is available this coming Thursday at nine a.m. (Always have a specific date and time available.)

The End.

Two things might happen:

1) The prospect will say Thursday doesn't work, in which case you find a mutually convenient time.

2) The prospect raises either a condition or an objection.

A **condition** is a characteristic of the prospect which impacts your ability to meet, and about which you can do absolutely nothing. They might say:

- we're closing up shop tomorrow, or

- we never have and never will use outside vendors for your line, or

- we're going to have a new owner next month and have been instructed to cut off all contact with prospective vendors.

Some conditions mean cross this prospect off the list ("going out of business"). Some conditions mean say good-bye and reschedule a follow-up ("getting a new owner"). All conditions mean move on to the next call, now.

An **objection** has been described as "an unsatisfied need couched in an emotional statement." This is a useful idea. It underlines the notion that the prospect could very well be in need of our service or product, but that he or she is stuck in resistance mode by an emotionally-based reluctance to overcome inertia and meet with this persistent, competent-sounding sales nut. The comfort zone is cozy. We can deal with this.

I have to say it again. We have but one goal: to get an appointment. We've given our *brief* introduction and are waiting, pencil poised, to fill in the meeting slot. We get an objection.

From a Redmond Group 2010 Sales Coach Newsletter:

OVERCOMING OBJECTIONS

Recently stated at a webcast by a sales consultant:

- Objections are a natural part of the sales process
- They only occur 100% of the time
- And only at the beginning, middle and end of the sales cycle.

I then added, "Embrace them."

I don't know about you, but I'm thinking my life would be better without objections. "Embrace them"—I don't think so. I mean, really, wouldn't things be easier if every prospect agreed with whatever we presented and couldn't wait to sign on? That's for another workshop. In the meantime, "Earth to Tom."

We didn't know this, but the word "objections" first entered the English language in the 14th century. I guess there were no objections before that, but I digress. Check out the Top Ten insurance-related objections at the bottom of the newsletter.

So how about a process to overcome objections? A formal definition might be helpful: *An objection is an unsatisfied need usually couched in an emotional statement.*

...and the overall process to overcome an objection in five steps is:

1. Diffuse the emotion back to a neutral state
2. Uncover the unsatisfied need
3. Respond
4. Verify

---

5. Move the process forward to the next objection or action step.

Now let's drill down:

1. Diffuse the emotion back to a neutral state

- Listen to the whole objection. What a concept!
- The sale has now stopped! Be mindful of this—the sale is over at this point.
- Step out of your role of a professional salesperson. Human to human communication is required.
- Pause; take a breath; think great thoughts and consider your response. The mind is incredibly fast—let it work for you.
- What did you see? What is the prospect doing as they are offering objections? What clues are in front of you?

Action steps:

- Offer a statement of GENUINE empathy.
- You are acknowledging the objection, not necessarily agreeing with it.
  For example:
  "I understand that…"
  "I hear that quite a bit and…" (My personal favorite)
  "I've heard that before…"
  "That must be very frustrating for you when…"
  Be careful with humor, but it can work: "Don't hold back, what do you really mean?"

Warning #1: PLEASE SKIP THIS STEP! If you are unable to offer a statement of GENUINE empathy (and some people just can't do it), you will just make matters worse.

2. Uncover the unsatisfied need

Follow up your previous statement with a question. Drill down about the objection. What are the underlying drivers behind the objection? Is there a hidden objection? What is the real objection? Two or three questions should be all that is needed to come to an understanding.

"May I ask you why that is important to you?"

"That's interesting; can you tell me more about that?"

"Some additional details would be helpful; may I ask you a few questions?"

Warning #2: There is a very strong tendency to skip this step —we typically want to go right for the solution.

- Our solutions
- Our brilliant ideas!
- Our incredible products
- Our exceptional services
- The wonderment of the technical aspects of our offering
- After all, it is all about us!

3. Respond

Now is the right time to bring your product, service or other resources back into the conversation.

- How does your product, service, organization or team respond to the newly discovered unsatisfied need?
- Detailed, specific response to the specific need is required here.
- Technical discussion is more than OK; now is the time for it.

4. Verify

Now is the right time to verify that you made a reasonable response. A question will help here:

"Does my explanation make sense?"

"Have I cleared up that misunderstanding?"

"Have I answered your question?"

"Will this make sense to the other people on your team?"

5. Move the process forward to the next objection or action step

You're now back to your plan; your presentation; your agenda. We're always looking for interesting objections—please send yours in.

Here are the Top Ten Objections for the insurance business:

1. We're not that unhappy with our current arrangements.
2. Our agent will fix what you tell us is broken.
3. I hate insurance.
4. What's so special about your agency, your company?
5. We only buy the least expensive insurance.
6. The coverage you're offering is too expensive.
7. The coverage you're offering seems too inexpensive.
8. You're too far away to handle our business.
9. I don't have the time to see you.
10. Just fax me the quote and I'll call you.
11. An appointment? How's never?
12. My brother, son, daughter, mother, father, etc. handles the insurance.
13. Oh, we already buy insurance.
14. What's your sign?
15. Don't worry; our building is fireproof.
16. I'm worried about changing our insurance to you.
17. I'm worried about changing our insurance to (Carrier).
18. Sure, come on in, we get quotes every few months.
19. I don't really need more coverage, i.e. umbrella.
20. Could you please provide us with another alternative? Five are not enough.

We couldn't stop at ten—at one time or another, every one of these objections has been presented to me. How about #14? You can't make this up. And a sense of humor is helpful.

Best wishes are flying your way,

Tom

We are not on the phone to make a sale. We're on the phone to make an appointment. Don't take anything personally. If the objections keep coming, then explain that your interest is in seeing if there's an opportunity to do some bridge-building. You want to be sure that you have the right equipment to handle the prospect's business and to make a substantial improvement in the current state of affairs. You have a long-term perspective. You're not on the phone to answer specific questions about product. It's not a dodge. Face-to-face is the proper venue for detail. Don't head down the path of too much information on the phone. "Let's talk about it. How's Thursday morning at nine a.m.?"

Confirm appointments a few days ahead of time. Many sales-people are reluctant to "rock the boat" and are fearful or supersti-tious about giving the prospect an opportunity to cancel a meeting. This is no longer tolerable as behavior befitting our value:

1) We're not supplicants who are lucky to be granted an audi-ence. We're bearers of valuable goods and services in a meeting of peers.
2) Our time is too valuable to risk on a trip to a missed ap-pointment; better to reschedule.

An Afterword

What looks like a daunting undertaking quickly morphs into another energizing feedback loop. As appointments get booked (and they will), we gain confidence in setting other appointments. New contacts become referral sources. The energy we apply to get-ting these meetings comes back to us in the form of unforeseen opportunities. Things change.

Most of your prospects appreciate what it's like to be in your shoes. As you maintain your professionalism, and stick (imperson-ally) to the game plan, you're going to win some of them over. It just happens. Getting appointments for sales opportunities can be usefully thought of in terms of getting interviews for a job. The process deserves the same amount of care and preparation as landing an opportunity to advance your career. Each call is an opportunity to contribute to the fulfillment of your goals.

Oh, yeah! A sense of humor is helpful.

Check out one of our 2010 newsletters on this subject:

Calendar Management

Congratulations! We're recommending that we all take a vacation from being in the sales business. We are now in the *calendar management* business. Calendar management is not *time management*— time can't be managed anyway. But calendars can be managed. What we're really talking about is the process of *managing the calendar of your prospect*.

We have never seen a time when it has been so difficult, so challenging to actually reach people. This is quite understandable. Everyone who has a job has at least two jobs. Remember the days when we actually had assistants? Ahh, but I digress! Look at your computer screen—you probably have four or five programs open right now. Plus your communication devices that never sleep. All this noise results in a bit of madness.

We now compete for the time and attention of the people we wish to meet. Let's face it; if we can't get on the prospect's calendar, then they can't become a prospect. Duh, no kidding, Tom!

Do you know anyone who has a product or service so unique, so compelling, that they can get through every time—salesperson to decision maker? Yes, as difficult as this is to take—even with our extraordinarily stupendous proven service package of increasing client sales—even we struggle to get through the noise.

So, how can one deal with this challenge at the very front end of the sales process? We think that precision, creativity, sustained energy, joyful perseverance, and humor can help.

First, some facts:

- 86% of our phone calls now go to voicemail (so you better be good at it!)

- Obviously this means that only 14% go to either the gatekeeper or the targeted person.

- It takes only one minute and fifty-one seconds to leave a voice-mail… and yes, always leave a voicemail. We recommend that you get out of the "Do I leave a voicemail?" debating society—just leave it.

- The chances of a callback are close to zero. The response statistics may be a little bit better with e-mail, but not much above zero.

- It takes seven contacts to get to the wrong person!

…and yet the best sales professionals persevere—the best get through.

Here's a good one: have you ever said to someone that you actually did reach: "Could you please switch me over to voicemail? I don't know what to say." It gets a good laugh because everyone gets it—try it out for yourself.

Some strategies to manage the calendars of others:

Q: When is the best time to contact a prospect?

A: When you are conscious.

Q: How often should you contact the prospect?

A: Until they surrender.

Q: What is the second best sales book ever written?

A: Dr. Seuss' *Green Eggs and Ham*. Check it out—the message is inspiring. By the way, we hand out copies of this book at our seminars.

Q: What about gatekeepers?

A: Work with the gatekeeper—invaluable assistance and ulti-mately, your advocate. Take the time to learn his or her name. Just ask or say, "I don't know your name." Keep in mind that you will be making multiple contacts and will be greeting the gatekeeper in the future.

When leaving voicemails, and we mean multiple voicemails, here's some sample dialogue to consider. You can apply most of these principles to e-mail as well:

- "This is my attempt to get on your list of important people to talk to."

- "Would it put more joy in your life if you were to meet with (insert your name)?" Our thinking is "How can anyone say no to that?" We're not kidding; we use all of these methods regularly.

- "I'm going to be in your neighborhood—I REALLY am going to be in the neighborhood, I really really am—and hope that meeting with me could put more joy into your life, etc. How's Tuesday at 10:00 a.m.?" Many of us do a fair amount of travel, and it makes sense to manage the travel time in the most efficient manner. Another digression: a most frustrating thing for me is when I tell people I am going to be in the neighborhood and nobody gets back to me anyway. That's my frustration—but that's a different workshop.

- "I know I've been missing you, so I'm going to take a leap here and put you on the calendar. I will call you on Thursday at 9:00 a.m." Call at 9:00 a.m. on the dot and leave another voicemail. Rinse and repeat with humor, humanism and professionalism.

- If you get to know them a bit (or think that you do because you've left a number of voicemails), try, "You might as well give up. I'm going to contact you until you surrender."

- For a referral: "John Jones referred me to you, and if I don't contact you, John will kick my butt all over the county."

- OK, we admit it; we've tried sales by telepathy. Sounds like a great title for a sales book: *Sales by Telepathy: You'll Never Have to Make an Outbound Call Again!* That actually does sound like a book title with promise.

- What about regular mail, a/k/a snail mail? We're not opposed to regular mail. Give it a try. At least we know the mail gets through, but you must follow up your mailing immediately with a call or an e-mail—you need to contact them as they are opening the envelope.

A good rule to prospect by: Eliminate any emotional attachment that anyone will get back to you. This becomes quite easy after the first 100,000 unreturned phone calls.

We think we're right about this—you are competing for the time and attention of your prospect. Notice we're not saying a word about price, product offerings, qualification or closing techniques; just plain old connecting with someone, person to person.

If you have any other hints on how to get in the door, please tell us what you may have tried. Don't worry about giving away your secret formula. We have good news—you have an unlimited supply of prospects.

...and never stop believing that you will get through.

Best wishes are flying your way,

Tom

(Your Name), Inc. Sales Process

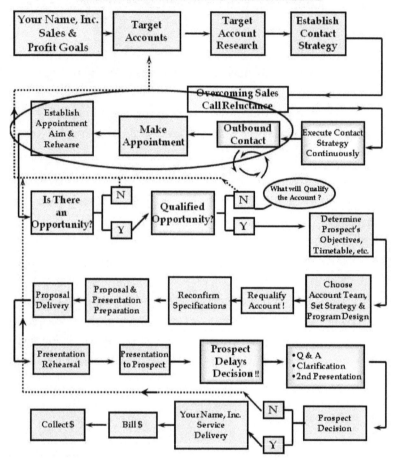

Copyright ©Redmond Group, Inc. 2011

Chapter 6

QUALIFIED OPPORTUNITY
You Want to Do Business with Me?

You have a meeting scheduled with Global Unlimited Power-house International (traded on the New York Stock Exchange under the symbol GUPPY). On the surface, you'd love to do business with them: they're a big buyer of what you sell, they're an innovator, a growing leader in their field, and they pay regularly and on time. Who wouldn't kill themselves to do business with Global Unlimited Powerhouse International? Maybe *you?*

Let's turn the question around. For all of their evident fabulousness, is Global Unlimited Powerhouse qualified to buy from you? You know who you are. You know your strengths and weaknesses. You have been following the map and have gradually realized the power that comes with sticking to your goal-setting regime, a regime that's separating you from the run-of-the-mill frantic and needy salesperson.

When you step into a meeting, your prospect is in the presence of a unique energy. She may not know exactly what she's up against, but we do. She's up against an integrated, fully developed, clean-burning, confident, focused, smooth-running energy source. You're drawing on your disciplined adherence to executing hand-written, living professional *and* personal goals. You're bringing your *entire* strength to the table. You're unfairly advantaged.

It's a privilege to buy from you. We don't bestow that privilege on just *anyone,* do we? Remember, the theme of the Sales Process Map is to make you more valuable than you already are. Care must be taken to release that value on appropriate outlets in the market. Your energy mustn't be frittered away. You know what you bring

119

to the table. How about Powerhouse? Are they a worthy recipient? And we know all about the pressure you're under, the pressure from your senior management to land this puppy—we mean Guppy.

Cost of Working on Unqualified Accounts

Before outlining attributes that serve to qualify prospects, let's take a look at the true costs associated with spending time and re- sources pursuing unqualified accounts.

Cost to You

You could be doing something else, like fishing, or shoeing a horse, or shopping, or playing ball with your kid, or working on a viable prospect, or taking a nap. It is way too easy to underestimate or ignore the cost of following the impulse that says, "Those people I just met were so nice! They *like* me! They laughed at my jokes! The sales manager's assistant's sister's ex-husband comes from the same town as my neighbor's brother's best friend's college room- mate! Can you beat that! It's a sign from above! What the heck, let's give them a proposal! They're a great company, and besides, we can do proposals in our sleep!"

It's hard to resist the satisfaction of feeling as though you've moved closer to the goal when you leave a feel-good, friendly meet- ing. But think about it. Most of us are reasonably civil, and a lot of us instinctively will try to make visitors to our office feel welcome. If a prospect has agreed to meet with you in their office, it's unlikely that they'll leap out from behind a hidden panel and hurl insults or a pitchfork in your direction as you enter the conference room. They're much more likely to be polite, maybe even *nice*, and willing to make some small talk while they listen to your pitch. *Nice* isn't a *sufficient* criterion for deploying forces. Beware of "happy-talk"; it's the enemy of information, and it can cloud the judgment of even the most experienced salesperson.

Time for a story. My colleague and I were visiting a prospective account for the first time. This account was just perfect for us —the correct size, location, terrific product and service fit—just right. We proceed with our meeting and the interview process and were able to sum up for the prospect their precise business objectives and how we might work together. So I asked something like, "If we're able to help you achieve your objectives, do you think we'll be able to do business?" The response was (I'm not making this up): "If you can achieve these objectives, YOU'RE THE MAN!" Believe me, these objectives were reasonable, and with some work, creativity and applied energy, the objectives were certainly attainable.

As we left the meeting, my colleague said, "That was a great meeting." My response was: "This is a dead end. We need to look at it this way: this prospect has been in business for something like 80 years. We meet with them for 90 minutes and 'YOU'RE THE MAN!'? They were just being polite."

Sure enough, the follow-up calls stopped being returned, the critical information never came through, and the prospect drifted off into the land that time forgot. So the next time a prospect says "YOU'RE THE MAN (OR WOMAN)," take this as a "no buy" signal and run from the account to a better one.

The "Qualified Opportunity?" square on the Sales Process Map is outlined in red. That means it's a decision point, a place where you stop and choose between alternative strategic directions based on an evaluation of input you've gathered in following the map to that spot. But let red also serve as a warning—it's also a breakdown in the sales process. "Perdition awaits ye who commit your own, your colleague's, and your company's resources to working on unqualified accounts!"

Let's assume you have an income goal. As you track your progress in fulfilling the monthly number of meetings and active proposals you'll need in order to hit your target, you'll quickly realize that there's no such thing as "just knocking off a proposal."

Anytime you're tempted to "just mark up an old presentation because *we can do it in our sleep*," then go to sleep instead, and take a pass on the presentation. Before committing to any presentation or proposal, serious effort must be allocated to an evaluation of the target.

Let's further beef up the concept of the active proposal to read active *qualified* proposal—a proposal that's in front of an attentive prospect, one who's in the market for what you offer, and who's prepared to buy from you. Proposals set adrift on a sea of "lottery ticket" hopes don't make it. They take you away from your goal. They're not harmless; they're deadly. Torpedo all derelict proposals this instant, and don't devote another thought to them.

(As your author re-reads these passages, I have to re-commit to eliminating unqualified prospects—right now. How did these unqualified prospects show up again? ...and I *teach* this stuff!)

We're starting fresh. *You're becoming a more valuable person*—more valuable to yourself, your employer and fellow employees, and your loved ones. This means that your time and energy have increased in value. They must be wisely spent. Working on unqualified accounts means you're undervaluing yourself and wasting precious, hard-earned resources. Working on the unqualified account is blocking you from working on the qualified account.

In a sense, it's like prospecting for gold. The way to increase the amount of time you're spending alongside a growing pile of gold dust is to let all of the pebbles and fool's gold drop to the ground, ASAP, and *move on* to the next pan full of potential. After all, there is an unlimited supply of potential accounts—you cannot get to them all. If you're in doubt about this "unlimited supply" concept, please take a moment and consider the accounts that you do not have.

Cost to Your Team and Your Company

Here's something that's (hopefully) painful to think about. It would be bad enough if it were possible for you to waste your time in pure isolation. But that's not the case. There's an exponential negative effect in chasing phantoms. Each pursuit of an unqualified account takes with it your human resources (members of your sales team, clerical support, research, marketing, administration, building maintenance…), hard costs (equipment, paper, postage, FedEx, IT, light bulbs, Post-its…), and precious travel choices.

Then there's momentum. Every choice to go after a prospect releases potential energy in the form of a giant boulder rolling downhill (the boulder is made out of the resources mentioned above—and other stuff, coming next). It's impossible to recover that energy once the boulder has spent it. It's *very* difficult to stop the boulder, and it requires lots of energy. Additionally, each time you remobilize after a failed shot, there's a danger of carrying some of that failure forward.

As positive, Zen, and forward-looking as you might be, it will always be easier and more fun to go after business when you consistently give each pitch the care and discrimination commensurate with its true costs. You're creating an environment of positive momentum for your team, rather than a hapless "hit or miss" attitude.

The rolling boulder also includes your (and everybody else's) expectations and emotional investment. You can't win 'em all, but don't underestimate the cost of recovery when eying a prospective deployment of forces, and remember that the cost goes beyond you. You want to stay in the groove like a consistent hitter, choosing your pitches, so that you cut down on the number of wild swings. They're hard to pull out of. Team morale builds when everyone feels that he or she will never be used as cannon fodder for somebody's whimsical, "what the heck" wild grab at unlikely business. Collective disappointment is a cost that deserves a lot of focus and forethought. *Get input from teammates* on account qualification; it can be turned into a powerful cohesive force for team building.

Time for another story, and maybe even an insight! Circa way back in the last century, our team was deciding whether to work on Project "Humongous." This one account, if landed, represented over 90% of our annual goal—a true giant. My inside information was that we did not have a realistic opportunity on this account, at least for this year. So I brought the team together and told them that we could not win this year, but we might be able to win "Humongous" in three years. Could we look at our time, money and effort spent as an "investment" in our future?

The team agreed to move forward, but knowing them well, I offered a word of warning: "During our work on this project, we are going to get excited about the possibility of landing the account and we're going to come up with some great ideas, some creative insights and strategies—even ironclad reasons as to why we should be hired. As a word of warning, in ninety days, when we do not get hired, I don't want anyone on the team expressing disappointment and uttering, 'We really are losers!' We're not going to land this account."

When we did not land the account, I reminded the team of our earlier conversation. An interesting insight was that we learned a lot from the "Humongous" experience and used that additional knowledge on other opportunities. The investment ultimately paid off well in ways we could not foresee. We learned about ourselves and used these insights on other opportunities.

Cost to the Market

Habitual qualification of opportunities has a positive and appreciated effect on that other crucial component of the sales machine, *your* suppliers. If you're an insurance agent, the suppliers are your underwriters; if you're a commercial real estate broker, the suppliers are the landlords; if you manufacture finished goods, the suppliers provide the raw materials. *Consistent qualification of opportunities will make you into a market energizer instead of a market sinkhole.*

You are competing for the time and expertise of your suppliers. Don't be the one who cries wolf more often than you produce viable opportunities. You often need information from suppliers to help you make a meaningful proposal. Let them know that you appreciate them by presenting a high percentage of real opportunities. As you succeed, they succeed; it's a high power feedback loop. Beware! The waste of the unqualified runs downhill.

Your sphere of influence goes way beyond you. "Qualified Opportunity?" is where you transfer strength from the powerful personal foundation you've built with goal-setting and pass it on to your co-workers and the marketplace. It's the filter that ensures a high return on your personal investment. The more valuable you become, the more you'll appreciate the value of others, and the more sensitive you'll become to the allocation of everyone else's resources.

Don't take your need to be busy and frenetic out on the marketplace. Realize the extent to which your prospecting can invigorate and resound throughout the whole food chain. Qualifying accounts produces big, positive resonance throughout your whole market. Great qualifiers protect their ability to do the next deal with colleagues, markets, suppliers, etc.

Cost to the Prospect

Don't waste the prospect's time. They may not fit your standards, but that doesn't mean you should burden them with an "air ball" proposal. They're likely to remember the salesman who says, "Thanks for the opportunity, but I can't help you with this one, good luck!" Care must be taken to *depart via the high road and keep the door open* for a future qualified opportunity.

Take a chance on demonstrating selectivity in choosing your potential customers. X number of prospects will be more impressed by a vendor who takes a confident pass on an opportunity than by someone who seems willing to indiscriminately run with the herd. And it's X that you'll want to do business with down the road, not the one who feels as if he's doing his job by collecting as many proposals as possible. It's a small world; you will likely see the prospect again under different circumstances. Count on it that something is bound to change at the prospect, in their market, with their current relationships, etc. It doesn't hurt to be remembered as discriminating and professional.

Establishing Qualification Standards

Now that we're forewarned, and have solemnly foresworn off the lethal pursuit of unqualified accounts, let's identify those characteristics of potential buyers that will help us stay on target and keep us in the pool of the qualified—where the winners are, where the wind blows free, and where our carefully cultivated resources are most likely to earn their proper return.

Webster's is always a good place to start. Hardly anyone ever says, "According to Random House…" Webster seems to be winning the "quotable-definition-provider-brand" category, but we digress. Webster defines *qualification* as "…a condition or standard that must be met for the attainment of a benefit." We're talking about qualifying buyers of our goods and services. The prospect must meet the "condition or standard," and one of the benefits attained by a qualified prospect is the privilege of buying from us! A qualified buyer gets *us and our energy and creativity and terrific services* as the prize. The qualified buyer attains the benefit of having us as a vendor. As pointed out at the beginning of this chapter, GUPPY has to pass muster with us, not the other way around.

If you are experiencing an inner voice of "what a load of crap" at this point, you are right on time. Please press on—don't stop now. And you don't want to miss Chapters 7 and 8. I can hear the voice which says, "Global Unlimited Powerhouse calls the shots. They hold the last card. The hire is their call. It's obvious. The seller is the supplicant!"

The "Qualified Opportunity?" square says that we're going to spend our resources (our caringly bred and increasingly powerful resources) on opportunities that meet certain standards. We're not going to win every pitch we make. But we're going to aim toward the best targets, keep ourselves in the highest probability zone and swimming with the right kind of worthies—quality companies that will give us an open shot at winning their accounts. They must be companies and individuals that are truly ready to allow us to help them make the transition to (drum roll...) *us*.

The law of large numbers is on our side. There's enough opportunity out there to allow us to pick our shots and never worry about running out of targets. We're the prize. Webster had the shoe on the right foot. From the minute we make the first call, through initial meetings, follow-up meetings, proposals, presentations, you name it, we're helping them to *transition to us*. That's our mindset from the get-go.

We're even going to provide the transition plan. When we hit a wall in the hiring process, we stop and divert that energy to a living Transition to Us Assistance Program. That stop order might come after the first meeting; it might happen with a blue-chip like Global Unlimited Powerhouse International.

And speaking of prizes:

Q. Which Webster wrote the dictionary? Daniel or Noah?
A. Search me! I'm just a nationally-renowned sales consultant.

Let me know if you find out. E-mail your answers to tom@ redmondgroupinc.com. Prize: your own copy of the number one sales manual of all time (and it is not this one yet).

Wow! Interactivity and valuable prizes! We told you this was cutting edge stuff.

Qualification Standard—Doctor/Patient Relationship

There's an important general attitude that should permeate a relationship with a prospect if you're going to help the company to hire you. The prospect should be willing to allow you into their world. You're the doctor. How can you diagnose and heal and comfort without the patient disclosing a lot of history and description of current conditions?

But sometimes patients are reticent. Try to determine if it's reluctance that can be overcome, or "waste of time" reluctance, where they're masking the fact that there's no business to be had or that the individual you are dealing with is not capable or desirous of beginning to move toward a transition *now*.

You need to make the judgment call as to whether the prospect is displaying any enthusiasm to hire you. Based on the old adage that the purpose of the first meeting is to get the second meeting, we would allow two meetings to give the prospect a chance to demonstrate that you are really in the door. If the first meeting is devoted to establishing your qualifications to handle the business, the second meeting is their turn to open up. Please note that the reverse order is OK with us as well—get to know them first, then it's your turn. Better yet, a give and take at every meeting is usually ideal.

When you schedule the follow-up meeting, make it clear that the agenda is to give *them* the opportunity to receive a head-to-toe examination. You are there to determine if there is a bridge to build between your companies. Alternatively, what are the factors that are preventing this bridge being built?

So what are we looking for? What is it that the prospect can let us in on that will indicate an open door for us to walk through and help them transition to us?

Qualification Standard—Why Are We Here?

Are there problems to be solved? Salespeople seem to be genetically afflicted with the belief that they can create deals out of thin air. I think it's a mutation of the recently identified "fools rush in" gene (it's located on the DNA strand right next door to the "I think I'll bang my head against this brick wall" gene). Maybe it happens from time to time. Maybe there's a particularly brilliant, clairvoyant and persuasive dealmaker who can spot a whale where no one else sees the signs, and pull down a huge sale where no other vendor, let alone the buyer, could even see a need. That may happen. But the highest frequency of sales is right out in the open, where the buyer sees a need, not where the seller has to convince the buyer of a hidden opportunity.

Got time for another story? In one of my past lives, as sales manager, we had developed the top ten criteria to qualify prospective accounts. Things like: Are they broke? Are they suing us? Can we do the job? etc. The tenth item was: "How desperate are we? Let's work on this account anyway; at least we'll look busy!" This is the Zen of sales: "Look busy, do nothing."

Radical Notion #2: It's better to get in the way of a sale than to chase a sale. It's a great feeling to be crushed right in the middle of a collision between need and fulfillment of need. In order to get to that crossroad, the buyer has to show the way. This is a crucial indication as to whether the door is really being opened for you to be helpful, or whether there's a door there at all. The prospective buyer must be candid with you and specific as to:

1. Needs that you might help to fulfill
2. Shortcomings in the current provision of goods or services
3. A question of an upcoming policy or lease expiration
4. The demands of a new product rollout
5. A serious interest in the utility of a product or strategy that's your specialty

In order for you to help them make the transition to your company, you need a toehold, a substantial insight into the whys and wherefores of their business model, and there has to be a hitch in the execution of that model that they need help in smoothing out. Don't be afraid of probing too persistently or asking questions if things don't make sense. Someone who can't or won't respond to reasonable clarifications about their current situation provides you with a powerful selection tool. They're not qualified prospects, and they are delivering "no buy" signals. Thank them and move on.

Remember, it's *you, your colleagues, and your company's valuable resources* that are in the balance here. If you're really going to be able to help the prospect, you need details: current pricing, contract expirations, product specs, service expectations, relationships with current providers, etc. If someone expects you to muster resources (for example, to provide a proposal or price quote), then during or certainly after the meeting, you should be able to summarize with precision what it is the prospect needs—their objectives.

Evaluate the degree of necessity and whether they have identifiable and achievable objectives. Is it something they'd *like*, or something absolutely essential to the maintenance and improvement of their business? Don't overlook the personal needs, the personal objectives of the buyer or buyer team. These could be of an even greater value and determinant of the decision than the corporate objectives.

In our experience, there is a weakness in the sales system across the country (and maybe around the world). Here it is: *identification, quantification, definition of their objectives*. In our workshops and during our speaking gigs, when we ask this question to sales professionals, "What are the objectives of your prospect?" the response (only 100% of the time) is focused on what we can do for the prospect. For example, save money, offer better service, fix a technical issue with their current arrangement and so on.

What we're really asking is, "What are the business objectives of your prospect?" For example, if they're a bus company, their objective is to get more butts in the seats; a building developer, to get more paying tenants; the state of Connecticut (or one of the other 49 plus territories and countless municipalities), to attract and retain residents and businesses. Get to thinking this way—what are the business objectives of your potential customer?

Here's some more free stuff! Your assignment is to determine three of five objectives for each one of your prospects—and you get two objectives for free!

1.
2.
3.
4. Your proposal must be competitive in pricing and terms
5. Your commitment to proactive service from you and your team

The next time you come across a prospect that wants high prices and poor service, please let us know. With effort we can deliver that!

Qualification Standard—Relationships

What's your relationship with the prospect? Is he forthcoming and candid about the business at hand? Does she seem uninformed or evasive? People with the greatest responsibility are often the least defensive when addressing the anatomy of their company, its strengths and weaknesses, industry trends, and the layout of their current and future competitive battlefield. After all, they have a lot of responsibility and are paid to get results. They generally appreciate and are on the same wavelength with other professionals who demonstrate concern with thoroughly understanding the context of the situation under study—remember our discussion on objectives? The greater effort you make to develop a deep understanding of the prospect's business model and the challenges she sees in front of her, or looming just down the road, the less likely you'll be to waste energy on a phantom, and the more confident the prospect will feel that she's not going to get a pre-fabricated proposal.

Reminder: it doesn't help to view the individual as only a cog in the corporate wheel. She has ambition, insecurities, ego, dreams, loved ones, other interests, pets, you name it. In the same way that you're bringing a self-consciously integrated package to the table, never forget that the person opposite you is, perhaps unconsciously, an integrated package too.

It has become a bit of a cliché (perhaps a useful cliché) to ask, "Where do you see your company in five years?" How about asking the individual where she sees *herself* in five years. You might find out that she has tremendous ambition, is well-connected and is a good horse to run with. Remember that your job is to help *her* achieve *her* goals, not to only help the "company" in some abstract sense.

On the other hand, you might find that he is a "clock-watcher" with one foot out the door, not someone likely to help you advance your cause, and not someone who's really clued in to important characteristics or decisions. In that case, the most he might possibly be able to do would be to point you toward the place where decisions are made.

People on the outer edge of the loop are usually the least inclined or the least able to open up. Certainly one area of information we want to examine with our prospect is how he fits into the decision making process, who else is on the team, how the process unfolds over time, and what milestones are involved. These are fair questions on your part. If you're going to allocate significant resources to outline and price a solution to the prospect's problem, then you need to know how your "baby" is going to be handled: what presentation format should it take and to whom should it be addressed, who should be there, who should be copied? What are the mechanics of the review process? When can you expect a face-to-face meeting for feedback and clarification with the *full* project team? You'd hate to see anyone left out. You don't want any concerns left unspoken.

You must be reasonably sure of feedback that's equivalent to the heft you bring to the table. You might consider offering insight into your own internal resources, their allocation and the decision procedure behind your choice as to whether to proceed with a project. You might also mention the players (bios to be included in presentations) on your team who'll be involved, and you'd appreciate bios of their team members. Bios can be incredibly rich sources of information on, for example, previous employment, schooling, and association membership. An inability to derive this degree of decision-procedure information from a prospect, including their team, puts them in the land of the unqualified and you in the land that time forgot.

Another relationship issue touches upon the prospect's current connection to his supplier or agent, your competitor. Where is the current supplier's connection? Is the person sitting in front of you the same one who hired the existing supplier? Could he fire the current provider? If not, then who could? (A good way to probe for the real decision-maker.) What's wrong with the current supplier? How long have they been in place? How did the relationship begin? Does the supplier have an extra-curricular relationship with someone at the top?

"Oh! You say your supplier's an ace golfer who plays weekly with the chairman? How great!" (I'll keep an eye out for the chairman's retirement announcement.) "Gotta go! Good luck on your project!" You don't earn extra fees for attempting or even winning near-impossible accounts. Try to stay on the fairway, the high probability zone.

Qualification Standard—Technical Ability

Is the prospect's dissatisfaction with the current arrangement based upon a substantial shortcoming in the provider's ability or inclination to fulfill the ongoing demands of the account? Are they able to meet the prospect's technical demands for specific products or services, delivered on time? Is there any obvious reason to suspect that your company can do the same job in such a remarkably new manner that the prospect will be willing to go through the inconvenience of transition? If you don't honestly believe that your technical and service capabilities are markedly superior, it's an unqualified account.

DISQUALIFICATION STANDARDS—WARNING SIGNS
⊗ X BEWARE X ⊗

Disqualification Standard—The Lost Sheep

The flip side of the qualification standards warrants some re-iterated additional surplus repeated overemphasis (this statement came directly from our department of redundancy department). When you sit down in front of a prospect, you should be focused from the outset on shepherding that person or persons on a transition from their current supplier to your company, like a sheepdog. Did you ever try to prevent a sheepdog from following its instinct to corral, coax, cajole and lead? Good luck. They'll run back and forth and circle and try to push around a pack of motorcycles if there are no sheep around.

You don't have to raise your back, bark, or bite the prospect's ankles. But you should have that shepherding instinct front and center in your consciousness from the outset. It will guide you and the prospect, and shape a mutually beneficial and informative session. Remember, you're there to provide a service—relieving the competition of the burden of their business. Transition is your goal, guideline, and mantra. You should probably try to manifest the instinct on a more cerebral level than a collie usually employs. No growling or baring of teeth!

You're not there to make friends (that may come further down the road, after you get the business). On your initial canvass call or mailing, you didn't start out by saying, "Let's be friends!" Presumably you're there to discuss the solution to a problem. If you can't steer the prospect away from "happy talk"—things like "how about them Yanks!"—then you're getting a serious warning.

There are plenty of people who will agree to meet with you out of some general sense of curiosity, boredom, or the need to show their colleagues that they occasionally have visitors. Such people are never the decision makers and probably don't know what issues are really under examination by top management. If you get the "not seriously engaged" signal from the prospect and you're not able to at least determine where decisions are really made, then cut your losses. This sheep's not qualified for, or ready to receive, the benefit of your guidance and protection.

Disqualification Standard—The Fisherman

Here's a dangerous character. Maybe his boss has said to him, "Why are we working with Acme? My son-in-law heard that they're pricey. And didn't they mess up the last order?" Or maybe he just feels the itch to allay his job insecurity by making sure that a current supplier doesn't make a fool of him by overcharging or skimming on service. Then you call. Great! Sure he'll meet with you! And up on his wall goes the "Gone Fishing" sign. The fisherman is afraid that he's being overcharged for something or that he's not getting enough for what he's paying. That's a fair concern. Bless his little heart. But he's not a qualified buyer.

There's generally an imbalance in the information exchange with the fisherman. He's really not that interested in hearing about your qualifications; he's not forthcoming on problems that you might help to solve; he's not inclined to provide any insight into his company's decision-making process. But he *is* interested in what a vaguely described job would cost, or how much other people in the building are paying in rent, or what your rate for such and such might be. There's a barely concealed hunger for a ballpark number, often wrapped in an inordinate amount of "happy talk." Again, at least try to find the real decision maker. And if you can't, you'd be better off doing some *real* fishing.

Disqualification Standard—Take a Number!

In the acting business there's such a thing as a cattle call. It's when a public notice for auditions is posted and every eager, desperate, aspiring actor within miles shows up, hoping that this will be the big break. The only trouble is that the chances of actually landing a role from a cattle call are infinitesimally small. They might be held to help the actors' union say, "See! We give *everybody* a chance!" That's right—a chance to waste time.

There are corporate cattle calls too. Requests for proposals will be carefully prepared, spec sheets will be available, and *any* qualified vendor can step right up and take a swing at the big opportunity. Bruce Willis might call it *Just Fishing with a Vengeance, Part II*. If after a meeting, the prospect says, "There's a stack of specs on a table by the door; please take one," say thank you. Turn around. Start marching. Do not stop at table. Do not pick up specs. Pick up overcoat and hat. Put on overcoat and hat. Do not look back.

It may be worth your while, when you get to your office, to try to meet someone a couple of levels above Mr. Spec Sheet. There you might be able to find out what's really going on and whether there's a worthy audience for your efforts. Remember, you're working hard to become more valuable. That value is nurtured in the proper environment. The proper environment is where there's a fighting chance to initiate a transition to your company. A lottery ticket or open auction is not a fighting chance.

Gut Feelings/Subtle Signals

We hereby give you permission to use your gut, your instincts as to the qualification of an account. And get this: you do not have to be able to explain your gut feelings—you probably can't anyway, at least not right away. Ever work on an account, and everything looks right, and yet there is some underlying gut feeling that says "run!"? And after you don't get the account, have you said to yourself something like, "I knew I was right, I knew there was something that would keep us from winning!" If you have not had this experience, you will.

Certain tried and true guideposts have been discussed to keep you moving in the right direction toward transitioning a qualified prospect to doing business with you. But we're not automatons.

Things never work out in neat patterns. There's always room for your gut feelings to play a part, while you're being careful not to let your gut consistently override standards. It can be a tough balance.

Be in harmony with these signals. You may have passed through a couple of meetings with your prospect, and:

- they've opened the door or you opened it for them,

- there's an evident issue—they need help that you're qualified to provide,

- you're working with the plugged-in decision maker,

- it's business you want and are able to handle,

- you've been given the green light to analyze and prepare a proposal.

But something doesn't feel right. Weird patterns start to develop. There are missed calls or appointments. Maybe calls are only returned after your business hours. Or your calls are only responded to by e-mail. You can't get the prospect to provide needed information. It feels as if your enthusiasm for the project is not nearly matched by the time and energy your prospect allots to it. Pay attention to your discomfort with these signals. You may choose to "stop the presses" on your efforts and try to determine if there's anything behind these behaviors.

You may find that the circumstances have nothing to do with you. Your client company may be distracted by an acquisition. Maybe they're being acquired. You may find that your contact is looking for a job. Or that there was a crisis that drained management time and attention, and soon everything will be all right. You might find that you're mildly paranoid and should see a shrink (in such cases, looking back, you'll often find that your spouse, kids, friends, and pets have been trying to tell you that for years).

The point is, keep your finger on the pulse of the relationship on an ongoing basis. As salespeople, we may not want to acknowledge that things change when we're in the hunt on an account. You want to cut down on the number of surprises that translate into an energy drain. *Pay attention to your gut.* There are times when it's beneficial for you to end a relationship *after* you've leapt through the first fiery hoops.

Accessory to a Transition

Have you ever said to your prospect, "You have lots of skills, but hiring us is not one of them"? How often do they change suppliers? It's not something that they do often, and certainly not for fun. So give them a hand—they need your help.

Remember, our conscious position from that first phone call, that first contact with a prospect, is that we're in the process of transitioning the account from their current vendor or agent to us. From your earliest discussions through your final proposal, transition should be a key element, right along with costs, specs, timing, and staffing.

The most successful sales professionals follow a systematic process in preparing the client to hire them. Here's another assignment: prepare a one-page flow chart that details a timeline and critical path for a smooth transition. It serves at least three purposes:

- It warms the prospect up to the notion that a time is coming when they will have to fire their current vendor, and there you'll be! We prefer that you use the word "fire" rather than terms like "transition" or "terminate your relationship with your current supplier." Here again is an example of caring for your prospect. They need to know that they will have to fire someone. If they cannot, we respect this and move on—another no-buy signal.

- It demonstrates the level of service that they will receive when they become a client.

- It *can* be traumatic to go through the transition. The chart will reassure them that you've orchestrated the operation many times and that no detail will be overlooked, including notifications, billing procedures, customer service contacts, account representation and such.

Please refer to our website, www.Redmondgroupinc.com, for a downloadable one page Transition Chart that should be used with prospects as early as possible in the sales process—even at the first meeting. Plant the seed. Mighty oaks from little acorns grow.

(Your Name), Inc. Sales Process

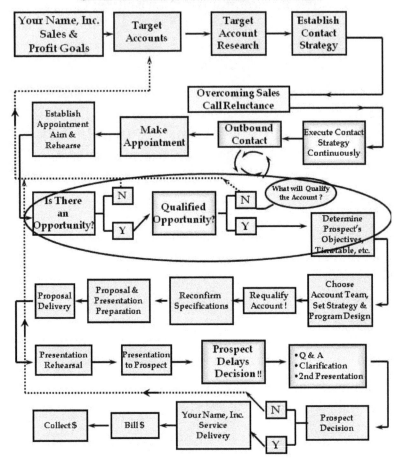

Copyright ©Redmond Group, Inc. 2011

Chapter 7

HOW TO GET AN ORDER, PART I
You Really Want to Do Business with Me?

Okay. Let's go after an order. You've arranged an appointment. This appointment is one link in a series of steps. It WILL have a direct impact on achieving a portion of your financial target. It WILL contribute to your overall increased value:

- through the acquisition of useful information

- by sharpening your skills as an effective kick-ass presenter

- by imparting critical information and insights to the prospect

- by illuminating an unqualified opportunity

- by saving your energy and redirecting you (and your team) toward a more fruitful expenditure of time and energy.

It's best to avoid the sense that you've carefully followed the Sales Process Map to this point and that you're now at a "Yikes! The big audition!" precipice. All the squares on the map are about the same size (a little tinkering with word processing could make them *exactly* the same size). You're in a *process* of coordinated steps. Each step has unique characteristics, but together they form an integrated whole. It's the whole that we're riding. Stay with the *process*. Don't skip a step; know where you are at all times.

"How to Get an Order" is a vital subset of Qualification on the same path. But you must be careful to see it for what it really is: a natural, conscious outflow of your personal and professional goals. You're building a methodical step-by-step process on the foundation of personal and professional goal achievement.

There may be a tendency to treat the actual face-to-face with a prospect as if it's some sort of pinnacle, a make-or-break test. This idea needs to be de-fanged. With the guidance of the Sales Process Map, you're developing a calm and powerful presence in the market. Still waters run deep. The appointment is *part* of the whole picture. Its integration with the rest of the picture is where it gets its strength. A smooth and steady strength, not a noisy "Do you like me? Please, please buy some of my stuff!" nervousness.

Think about the approach you took in Chapter 2, "Targeting Prospects." You stepped back and got a handle on who *you* are, as an individual and as part of a living mechanism of experiences and influences. You looked at the *prospects*, not as individual points on a vast landscape, but as components of their own extended living system. You bring a lot to the table. And your prospect brings a lot to you. Financial reward is only part of it. It's a part you're most likely to experience when it takes its proper place—service to your personal and professional goals, and service to your customer. When you enter the room to meet the prospective customer, develop the habit of thinking in terms of *all* that you embody, personally and professionally. Take a peek at your goals before you head into the meeting.

Remember Chapter 5, "Appointment Making"? Now to the street. You worked on the idea that you don't, for example, take cold calling personally, you just do it. *Your strength and sustenance comes from within, from your focus on goals and the execution of this proven linear process.* You don't get into wrestling matches with voicemail contraptions. You don't look to gatekeepers to fortify your sense of self worth. You just *do*. Impersonally.

When you get to the point where you're providing valuable service to a customer, *then* you can take things personally. You want to preserve that sense when heading to the actual appointment. You've already done some fundamental, value-enhancing self-redirecting before you step out on that sales call. You've done some research on the prospect. Make sure you don't leave it all behind. The appointment is one step among several on the Sales Process Map. It's part of a continuous systematic process, not an isolated test.

And What About That Appointment?

In addition to its place on the Sales Process Map, the appointment is a component of the metrics previously established as part of your process of reaching personal income goals in Chapter 1. You established a relationship between the number of new business meetings and the number of proposals made. In Chapter 5, you looked at the ratio between number of contacts and number of appointments. Chapter 5 says that the purpose of a contact is to get an *appointment*. Period. Similarly, the purpose of the new business meeting is to determine whether or not the prospect is worthy, and qualified, to receive a *proposal* from you now, in the future, or never. Period.

The purpose of a call is to get an appointment. The purpose of an appointment is to decide whether to muster forces for a proposal. It's that simple. You fortified your qualification standards in the previous chapter. The appointment is where you road test your qualification process. As a bright young Shakespeare once wrote: "To propose or not to propose, that is the question." (Or something like that.) Paraphrased from *Hamlet*, Act 3, Scene 1.

Focusing on the issues of qualification and weighing the merit of making a proposal produce side benefits that underscore the "whole is more than the sum of the parts" aspect of your approach. It enhances the value of the meeting for you *and* the prospect. It defines and raises the quality of your exchange.

Often, sales meetings play out on the level of a hearty "Hello" followed by an auto-pilot recounting, by the salesman, of why he and his company are unique and how they really give great service and how their prices are competitive, with a reference to the great companies he's helped and "Do you know So-and-So? I've known him for twenty years! Isn't he great?" and "How about those Steelers!" Most sales pitches are sleepers. They rate just below the plague in the minds of many prospective customers. The buyers have developed antibodies.

Happily, companies need goods and services. Somebody's going to provide them. The law of large numbers says that there'll always be a qualified buyer who's willing to hear what you have to say. The salesperson's focus on the prospect's qualification to be considered as an account and on their proposal-worthiness brings to the surface all of the energy you've been cultivating and places it smack in the middle of the conference room table, halfway between the potential customer and you.

Now you have an expanded appreciation of:

- yourself as targeter

- your wide survey of the landscape of potential recipients of your services

- the way you've come to view the concept *qualification* as an essential component of the *prospect's* characteristics

- your growing consciousness of the relationship between personal and professional goals

- the fact that you're sitting across from someone who might be able to fulfill *his* responsibilities more effectively through your service, your research—all of these things combine to give your appointment a distinct character. You will have a deeper meeting because you're looking deeper from a deeper place than the average salesman. Your approach informs your demeanor; you're not slick; you're not a supplicant. The prospect will sense that you're not interested in wasting your time *or* his time. It's a pro-to-pro meeting.

Rehearsal

Each step on the Sales Process Map deserves care and feeding peculiar to its own characteristics. The appointment is nurtured by rehearsal. A little pre-meeting preparation will serve to raise the chances that you (and the prospect) derive the greatest benefit from the encounter. You benefit by setting the bar at a level most likely to produce what you need to know in forming your evaluation of the proposal-worthiness of the prospective customer. The prospective customer benefits by introduction to a sharp, well-informed professional (not a time-waster) who might be of assistance in helping her to achieve the highest quality, successful execution of her responsibilities, and who seems prepared to do so.

Rehearsal can make the difference in producing these benefits, and in distinguishing you from the herd. You already have a reservoir of information to shape the specifics of the meeting. Look back to Chapter 2, "Target Prospects: Weaving the Widest Net." Under the subheading "Target Account Research," you've done some digging around the products, size, direction, growth pattern, and image of the prospect. You did that in the process of sifting through the universe of possible recipients of your goods or services. The work is already done. Now it can be recycled to give substantive shape to your meeting.

Look back through your notes. Is there anything in the research that could be clarified by the prospect to advance a *meaningful* evaluation as to whether you can provide valuable service? Go to your IT department supply closet and grab one of those next-generation leading-edge high-tech implements: yellow pad and #2 pencil. Write down any clarifications about the prospect's market status and direction that will help you to further the cause of qualification.

Write down some open-ended questions that will get the prospect talking about his business. These questions might include things like the effect of off-shore competition, technological changes, demand-driven alterations in their market, economic recession, or the impact of financial regulatory changes. Where does he see the business in five years?

How does the prospect generate revenue? You might be thinking to yourself, "They sell air filters. Everybody knows that. What a stupid question. And to think I went to the trouble of getting Redmond to autograph his book." But the company does more than sell air filters. They sell to a certain segment of the market: maybe to household consumers, maybe to high-tech manufacturers in the semiconductor business, maybe to health care facilities, maybe to the automobile industry, maybe to NASA. So what? So maybe you get some insight into their way of looking at the world and how they sell, how they distribute air filters. Maybe you discover a connection to your own experience.

Such insights can help to tailor your proposal and presentations to a language and outlook that's most appropriate and useful to both of you. Beneath the surface, behind their product, there's a particular way in which they connect to the market, *their* market. A whole world of inner workings serves that connection. That's the real heart of the matter. A little warm-up might lead to a big discovery, an entry to that world—into *their* world.

It is more than helpful to rehearse these general and specific questions with a colleague or team member before heading into the meeting, maybe the night before, maybe on the drive from the airport. Work from the notes you just prepared. The rehearsal accomplishes several things. In running through topics with another person, you might uncover an idea or line of thinking that's illuminating. You might make a connection to a previous experience that could bear relevance to the meeting. You'll definitely feel more confident and at home than when you burst through the door on a "wing it" basis.

Rehearsal helps move the center of gravity away from you and how great you are, toward the unique challenges that the prospect faces. It promotes and demonstrates honoring the prospect's time (and yours). Rehearsal also enhances the probability of maintaining a favorable direction during the meeting by embedding, in your exchange, probes specifically aimed toward the uncovering of useful information.

But do not be a stiff. If the conversation takes a turn (and it surely will) that veers from your preconceived path, then go with it, of course, as long as it's generally heading in the direction of useful information. When it gets within ten miles of the last NFL season, then *gently* introduce something that furthers your qualification assessment. You'll have plenty of time to talk about football *after* you sign the customer to a contract. It's very poor territory for differentiating yourself on a first meeting. The easiest kind of superficial banter delivers exactly what you'd expect: superficiality. Your customer is demanding skill-based competencies—so stay focused.

You may find that they're not half as equipped to discuss your questions as you are to ask them. That's okay. Your gut feeling about the threadbare carpet was right. Before the meeting they seemed worth a try. But if well-informed questions are met with a blank stare, then you've learned something. Maybe you don't have a decision-maker. Or the business could be floundering. Here's where you may or will drop 'em into the "Unqualified," "Much Later" or "How's Never?" bin.

Before we go further, we have good news. There is a handy one-page "How to Get an Order" checklist at the end of this chapter.

Prospect's Objectives

Your research and rehearsal aim toward a goal: identifying, quantifying, and defining the prospect's objectives. Your prepared and rehearsed probes may uncover such objectives. But it's also possible that in the give-and-take of your exchange with the prospective customer, there remain certain core issues that require elaboration. They may even be concerns that are not "top of mind" to the prospective customer herself. There's a way to bring them to the surface, and in doing so, you enhance the value of the meeting for both sides.

Let's revisit a few ideas presented in Chapter 6, "Qualified Opportunity: You Want to Do Business with Me?" Under the sub-heading "Qualification Standard—Doctor/Patient Relationship," as previously discussed, a qualified account will let you into their world so that you can really understand their business and determine if there's an opportunity for you to elevate their competitiveness. Under "Qualification Standard—Why Are We Here?" you examined the notion that there must be a circumstance that needs improving, a need to be filled, in order to give solid form to a partnership. You also looked at "Qualification Standard—Relationship." A qualified account must allow you, through the effort of you and your team, to find your way along a clear path through their decision-making process. Relationships with existing vendors need to be understood. You're to bring all these qualification standards to the face-to-face appointment and test them.

At Redmond Group, we've conducted countless workshops (I suppose we could count them, but I digress) and asked the same question hundreds of times and have received an infinite variety of answers. The question is, "When you meet with prospects, what do you discover that they want from you as a vendor, product or service supplier?" The responses fall into a rather narrow grouping. They range from "lowest cost" and "best number" and "least expensive" and "price competitive," all the way to "superior service" and "proactive account maintenance" and "great support" and "attentive follow-up."

A veritable rainbow of customer objectives. In two colors—Price and Service. Occasionally you'll get fringe answers like "least monetary outlay" or that the customer wants "Johnny-on-the-spot post-sale hand-holding." No kidding. It happens only one hundred percent of the time.

But it's rumored, through ancient sources, that there might be more than two answers to your question. In a galaxy far, far, far away, or perhaps in another dimension. It would be a great discovery. It would open up a whole new range of objectives through which you could link up to the prospect, offer more in the way of specific service, separate yourself from the rest of the "price and service" horde (they represent ninety-five percent of the matter in the sales universe), and find a mutually-beneficial outlet for the unique energy you're developing.

Price and service are obviously key concerns that buyers face. They're so obvious and important that you don't get any points for giving them as answers to the "What are the customer's objectives?" query. They don't give you any useful information. In seminars, we introduce this topic by asking the audience to identify five major "objectives" that we (and you) run into when calling on prospective buyers. The hands all shoot up. I say, "And I'm going to give you two for free: competitive price and excellent service." The hands drop. By the way, if you find a prospect that wants high prices and poor service, even we can deliver (with effort)!

So everyone's experience uncovers the same two items, no matter what category they're selling into. That doesn't make sense. It can't be true that the owner of a keyboard assembly plant spends her time, day in and day out, with the same concerns as a hospital administrator or a furniture manufacturer. They each want to build brand strength, expand their reach, keep costs down, attract and retain employees, and grow margins. But those are general concepts. They don't give you a toehold.

Ask the prospect upfront to help you identify their expectations from a supplier in your business. After they say "low price and good service," then you can really start to get to the bottom of things. What you're after is an understanding of *their* perspective; you want to step through the mirror and see things from *their* point of view. They generate revenue by providing goods and/or services within a general category; within that category they have certain target niches and specialties. Their growth options lay in certain directions. Their competition is making certain moves. They sell in a certain way. They have a characteristic supply chain. New firms are entering and exiting their territory. New technologies are favoring or threatening their position. Hey, that sounds like every business, including your own!

In order to find a unique foothold for building a bridge to the prospect, you have to make an effort to see their *strategic* objectives, and their operational challenges and advantages. That's where the heart of *their* business beats on a day-to-day basis. That's where you want to secure your relationship.

Way back in the last century when I was in the commercial insurance business, I remember meeting with a major bus line. I asked them what their objectives were as they related to our business and our relationship. They responded that they wanted the best insurance coverage for the least amount of premium, and that they wanted great pro-active service from me and my team (I wasn't shocked!).

Then I moved the conversation around to their perspective as operators of a business. It isn't always easy to do. But remember the doctor/patient relationship. You have to get as far as you can into the history and current conditions that are special to *this* customer if you are going to provide unique, tailored, differentiated service, and deliver the appropriate product. If the prospect adamantly fends you off with, "Just give me a quote," that's a sign that you are in the land of the unqualified.

We're trying to get the word "quote" out of the vocabulary of business. We're failing, but we continue to try. Try substituting the term "proposal." You know this already—"Quote" is a number. "Proposal" is a statement of services, advantages, disadvantages, your commitments, etc. And yes, a number (price) is to be included. But it's way more than Price, Price and did I mention Cost? Start using the term "proposal" and watch your stature as a sales professional improve.

The bus company executives started to open up. There were obvious concerns, like "getting more butts in the seats" and route expansion, but as the conversation continued, we landed on customer and driver safety issues. This was an area where working with the insurance carrier in a meaningful way affects this critical concern and key operating feature of this potential client. In response, we incorporated equipment maintenance programs, specialized training, and continuing safety education into the insurance and risk management program. This would not only be of immense importance to passengers and employees, but would also produce, over the long haul, more customers in the seats as a demonstrable concern with safety became a substantive part of its brand. We became part of a beneficial strategic initiative. That's where you want to be.

Again, you've done some research before the meeting. Try to get those clarifications that, for your purposes, will help qualify or disqualify the prospect. You will automatically be probing for meaningful opportunities to build a bridge. Perhaps, when all is said and done, there doesn't immediately appear to be any direct link, like the safety program. It doesn't matter. An attempt at well-prepared, deep digging never goes to waste.

Try to understand the buyer's challenges. It differentiates you from the "How much do you want? This is how much it will cost" crowd. (Remember, that's ninety-five percent of the sales universe.) Many times a successful, long-term relationship starts with a prospect saying, "You know, nobody's ever asked me that before." You're looking for long-term, differentiated, high-quality relationships. They can be built only on a deep foundation. A deep foundation requires deep digging. And guess what fuels the backhoe? That's right—your goals.

The effort to build a relationship upon the unique characteristics and goals of a customer opens the possibility of moving your bond away from pricing as the paramount consideration. Commodities can be purchased from anyone, based on price alone. You don't want to be a commodity. It's a dull existence. The best way to avoid that deadly trap is to wrap your energy, creativity, expertise, products and services around achieving the vital objectives of the customer. The customer benefits, and you become an integral part of that benefit. Price is not the issue. Increased value is the issue.

Reminder: Even if you're not immediately able to identify that unique link, the effort in trying to understand the prospect's core objectives produces results. One result is setting you and your team on different footing. Additionally, you're going to gather information. You ask well-directed, informed questions guided by your evaluation of the prospect's qualification to work with you. Then you do a lot of listening.

An appointment isn't an opportunity to show off. It's an opportunity to learn. And to build bridges. The information gathered has utility well beyond the actual sale that's in front of you. You may learn of an industry trend, or discover a rising player in the prospect's category; you might learn of a pending merger in the industry. There's no limit to the potentially valuable nuggets you might pick up by guiding and listening.

As you rehearsed prior to the meeting, in part to enhance your focus, you were in the process of determining the underlying objectives of the prospect. Now borrow a concept from the development of your goals: specificity. You should understand the prospect's objectives with as large a degree of particularity as can be managed. A good way to imprint this degree of specificity is to strive to be able to restate the objectives in a quantified form, where appropriate. This would apply to goals of the prospect that can be reduced to measurable descriptions. For example: the number of new store openings or an aimed-for increase over existing passenger miles.

Where goals cannot be reduced to numbers, an attempt to define the goal in as simple a form as possible will accomplish the job. The point is, when you strike illuminating information during your appointment, don't let it pass by if you don't feel comfortable that you understand it thoroughly enough to enable you to quantify or define it with reasonable accuracy. Get clarification where needed. Buyers (and most anybody, for that matter) are more impressed by someone who asks questions when needed, than by someone who "uh huhs" their way through a meeting as if they already know all about the prospect's challenges.

Do You Have an Order?

You're consciously and steadily shepherding the prospect toward a transition to you, from even before the very first call, the first contact. During your appointment, you underscore this process. You have been listening. You've learned something about the characteristics of the challenges and objectives that concern the person sitting across from you. You've tried to steer the conversation in the direction of those features that are uniquely important to the competitiveness of the prospect.

Keeping your dialogue on the level of price and service alone won't lead to a deep enough view of the way operations really play out for the customer on a daily basis. You provide real value by attaching your product or service to specific facets and needs of the business. *Then* you can price them and outline a service program.

Now you take the position that you're on the road to a partnership (if they're qualified) by asking this question straight-out: "If we achieve these objectives (recite them), do we have an order?" Warning! Warning! This is not a script, this is a guideline—the dialogue has to be yours. The question has to be genuine, it has to reflect who you are, and it simply has to be asked.

The first benefit of asking the question is that it implies you're capable of defining and quantifying the objectives. It forces you to see if you really got the message. When you summarize the core objectives (you can leave price and service out; they're givens), you might get it right. That's great. Or you might find that the prospective customer says, "No. That's not exactly it. What I really mean is..." or "That's not as important as..." or "I forgot to mention..." That's even more than great. A degree of partnership is implicit in the prospect's clarification. By laying out the objectives as specifically as you're able, you start floating down a current toward transition.

The second benefit is that you place squarely on the table the married union of "objective" and "order." You're keeping a steady pressure on transition to you. You're there to get an order; the momentum must come from your side of the table. It is your responsibility to your goals.

If the prospect says something like, "Certainly. I don't see why not," don't roll your eyes or snicker to your teammate while you're still in the meeting room. Don't hit that *ka-ching* button! What you've learned is that it's now worth your energy to deploy a proposal. You're ready to move one step forward on the Sales Process Map.

Ka-ching—many of you can recall the sound of a cash register when they actually rang every time the drawer was opened awaiting a deposit of cash. In the sales game we call this the "ka-ching" factor. You know, when you can hear that sound even way before you actually have an order. We've studied this phenomenon and have fallen under its spell ourselves: "Oh, I know I have this one, it's as good as landed" or some such nonsense. Using a sports analogy, when you are under the spell of the ka-ching factor, you lose your fastball. You stop asking questions. You work on less qualified accounts because this one is in the bag. When you hear that sound, think of it as an alarm—an alarm that tells you that you are moving away from a close. The term originated during the Ka Ch'ing dynasty in China—an empire made up of failed salespeople. We made that up, but it still makes us chuckle.

After clarifying and even reinforcing the objectives, work out, in cooperation with the prospect, a preliminary strategy to achieve them. Obviously, it's not time to provide your game plan in any kind of detail. That comes later, when you reconvene to present your proposal. You can, however, outline in general terms the process that will be followed in addressing the solutions. Items to be covered might include agreement to:

- fix a date when *everybody* in the decision process will be available for your presentation

- agree upon the location and time allotment

- discuss the format and availability of presentation equipment

- request names of participants from the customer

- offer to provide a summary of your team bios as part of the proposal.

Set the ball in motion by agreeing upon the most general features of the process. That could include an expectation of a follow-up presentation to develop ideas that emerge during the first formal get-together. The idea is to give and take (listen), keep moving forward, and engage the prospect in a substantive, practical, goal-oriented direction for the next steps.

Who Determines if You Have Achieved the Objectives?

The appointment is the time to solidify a concept first broached in Chapter 6, "Qualified Account?" Try to pin the prospect down, with the greatest specificity possible, on how your achievement of the goals will be evaluated. This question reinforces the idea that you're focused on meeting certain objectives and that you're (rightfully) interested in understanding the processes and personnel that will combine to make the evaluation.

You might find out that there are other people from other divisions, departments or locations who are impacted by your service. You should request the opportunity to meet with them before submitting the proposal. If you don't ask the question, you might miss the opportunity to address a major concern that lies under a jurisdiction different from that of the person with whom you are meeting. How cool—more objectives to uncover and respond to.

You're talking about offering the best-informed and the most useful proposal. You're sensitive to being caught "going around" the point-person on a project. You're not talking about "going around" anyone. Ask how the process works, then ask if it might be beneficial to meet the different components of the process. If the answer is no, the answer is no. If the answer is yes, then you're on the way to more information and a step closer to becoming a "part of their team."

Can We Do Business Together? Take a Sounding

In our experience, we've encountered situations in which everything has moved along splendidly and we were more than hip-deep in preparing a knock-'em-out proposal. Then, in the course of phone calls, perhaps to set the presentation date or to verify a piece of information, we were told, "Oh, by the way, we can't do business with you. You service our main competitor. Sorry. Have a nice day." Gulp. It's no fun to get that phone call (e-mails are even worse!). A lot of psychic energy goes right down the drain.

So this question must be asked (again, this is not a script—the use of *your* language is critical): "Is there any reason you could not do business with our firm, our team or me?" You may not be able to uncover every single contingency and protect yourself against every possible unpleasant surprise. But this is a way to get some protection while at the same time engaging the prospect in taking a little mutually-beneficial sounding of your game plan. Encourage her to check with all parties involved in the decision to make sure that your initial course settings head for the right direction.

Arrange a phone date, perhaps a week after the initial meeting, to see if any of her colleagues might have some useful input. This seemingly unimportant procedure has merit on its own terms and the added great side-benefit of possibly smoking out any obstacles that didn't surface during the first face-to-face. It demonstrates your concern for thoroughness, spreads the influence of your new project a little deeper, and might just uncover a potential hitch, either giving you the opportunity to create a remedy or the ability to learn sooner rather than later that trouble's coming from some previously-unseen quarter.

It's Great to Be Working with You!

Two outfits may, at the same time, be vendors for the same goods and services to the same company. One example is a wholesale pool and spa distribution company. The company buys products from numerous vendors: two or three brands of pool heaters, pumps and filters, chemicals, winterizing pool covers, etc. They had to be selective, having to choose the two or three brands carried from the ten or more manufacturers who wanted their account. In some industries and in some business relationships, however, there's the little matter of replacing a single current supplier. Examples include a professional relationship with a law firm or representation by an insurance agency where a single service supplier is the norm.

In both cases, the underlying principle of your Sales Process Map is to accumulate momentum that builds to transitioning the prospect to you, acting as a single supplier or in a shared capacity with a competitor. You build from square to square and face (squarely) *everything* that crops up. You are able to anticipate things that are inevitable and have a strategy already in place. Thus, you're in the habit of making the delicate suggestion, at the first meeting (toward the end) that, of course, you're talking about *firing* the existing vendor(s). Please use the word *fire*, rather than, for example, *terminate*. It has a certain shock value that profoundly highlights an issue that's sitting (invisibly) right in the middle of the table.

By asking, "Do you see any issues connected with firing So-and-So?" you might discover any number of things. You might discover that So-and-So has thoroughly alienated everybody from top to bottom and that they're halfway out the door already (Uh, oh, is that "ka-ching" I hear ringing in the background?). Get this: that's a signal for you to *pay no attention* to that information and to proceed with as much energy as you would if So-and-So appeared immovable.

Their response might be, "I don't know. I didn't hire them." In this case, find out who *did* hire them, and if they're still around, do everything you can to make sure that they're involved in the process. You might make this subject a special element of the "sounding" discussed previously. Suggest that the prospect confirm with the person who hired the existing supplier that she's looking at a remarkably competent and fascinating new replacement (you). If there's a problem, it's better to find out while there's time to address and develop remedies in your proposal, or to determine that it's time to bring out the "unqualified" bin.

The "firing" question is another momentum-builder. It places a substantial issue on the table, a step that's essential to the transition. Introduced by you, it's something that links you to the gathering momentum and reinforces the sense of a developing partnership.

Accessory to a Transition

Have you ever said to a potential customer during an initial meeting, "You have lots of skills, but hiring us may not be one of them"? You'll make it easy; you'll show them how it's done. And you mean it. People don't change suppliers every day of the week. They do not have this skill—how could they?

Under the above section "Do You Have an Order?" you restated and clarified the prospect's objectives. Now you work with the prospect on outlining the general features of the transition steps to follow. Include in those steps a brief memo, to be provided by you, that will show that you understand the transition process from the existing vendor to you. There are certain things you and the new customer will have to learn about each other, and certain personnel, on each side, who will have to be introduced. There are, perhaps, inventories that will have to be liquidated or policies that will have to be cancelled or security clearances that will need to be procured. Sketch out the steps that need to be followed to result in a seamless change-over, with a timeline where applicable, to be delivered when you make your formal presentation. It's a vital and not often easy procedure for your customer. You have an opportunity to be of real service by being proactive in its implementation. And you, once again, underscore transition.

We have more good news; please refer to our website, www.Redmondgroupinc.com, for a downloadable one-page Transition Chart.

(Your Name), Inc. Sales Process

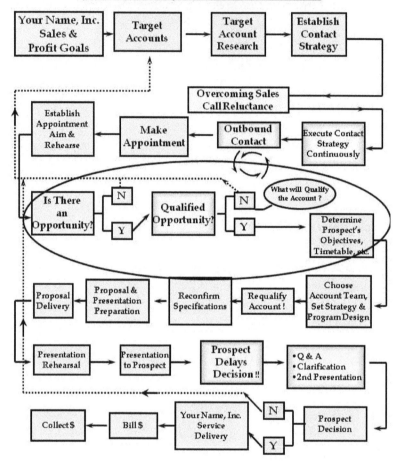

Copyright ©Redmond Group, Inc. 2011

How to Get an Order: Checklist*

Your prospects have lots of skills; hiring you is not one of them.

1. Identify, quantify, and define the prospect's objectives—we suggest five, and you get two for free!

   a.

   b.

   c.

   d. Competitive Pricing

   e. Exceptional pro-active services

2. Ask: If we achieve these objectives, do we have an order?

3. Ask: Who determines if we have achieved these objectives?

4. Ask: Is there any reason you could not do business with me, our firm, our team, etc?

5. Ask: Are you psychologically prepared to fire your current supplier?

6. Strategize with the prospect on how the objectives will be achieved.

7. Instruct the prospect in how to hire you—how to transition to you and your team.

8. Ask for the order often.

*Please note, this is not a script! These are guidelines. Use your dialogue, your internalized dialogue—*the genuine you* is the only thing that will work.

Chapter 8

HOW TO GET AN ORDER, PART II
A Building Project: Building a Team, Building Toward a Proposal and Presentation

Now the appointment is over. We have established that there is:

1) a qualified opportunity (an opportunity *you're* interested in pursuing),

2) the prospect is interested in receiving a proposal from you.

To say that an opportunity is qualified is a weighty statement. It means that it's a living chance to get us closer to our goals. It also means that we're ready to spend significant resources drawn from ourselves, our teammates, our employers, the market, and the prospect. There are no half-hearted efforts on the Sales Process Map. Even when we decide to take a pass on an unqualified customer, we walk away with determination, right back to the map and our guided hunt for targets more worthy of our attention. The emphasis is on building step by step to a grouping of rich targets. As an individual opportunity comes into focus, as measured by an evaluation of the content of an appointment, then we determine how to set up for our very best shot at converting the opportunity into a step toward goal-fulfillment.

For illustrative purposes, we'll assume that our follow-up with the prospect has two basic components:

- a proposal (under a format selected from a variety of possibilities: for example, hard-bound copy; DVD; Power-Point)

- a follow-up presentation of the proposal to the prospect.

Additionally, we'll assume that we put together a "team" of people to help us develop the proposal and to make the presentation. This scenario will bring to the surface many of our underlying emphases. Clearly, events don't always unfold in precisely this manner. But the basic ideas presented will serve to guide us as we continue along the Sales Process Map. You know this already, but the "team" could be just you. These items, the concepts, the format and the necessary activities apply equally.

Here's a simple idea to be wrapped around team assembly, proposal preparation, and presentation: everything we think and do in preparation and delivery of our proposal to the prospect rests on two notions: *transition* and *customer objectives*. These words lead the way, no matter how the follow-up plays out.

Operation Transition, Continued

Singleness of purpose has a way of organizing our energy expenditure with very little uphill climbing. Suppose someone were to ask you, "So… I understand you guys met with Acme Corporation yesterday, a great company. What's going on? Any business there? Any chance of winning it? What's next?"

You can *say* anything you want in response. But what you're thinking is, "What's going on? Next? Hasn't this guy read Redmond's book? We're transitioning Acme from their current supplier to us. And we've been doing it for a while, since the time they first emerged from our contact strategy. Yesterday's meeting just confirmed that we're all engines full ahead on the transition. Winning it? This isn't a lottery."

As you regroup after the appointment to sketch out your follow-up plan, everything you do, think and say is colored by the step-by-step transition of Acme to your book of accounts. If you were on an operating table, you wouldn't be too happy if the surgeon suddenly decided to jump ahead to the sutures without actually completing every single stage of the surgery with great care. Your goal (and hopefully the surgeon's goal) is that you emerge from the operating room with a greater shot at overall improved living conditions. The operation is a step-by-step process that follows that guiding objective. It's the same with the process of acquiring new accounts. There are no shortcuts, and there is but one framework that supports every move you make—transition to you.

Prospect's Objectives—The Ruler

"Ruler" is a great word. It has two perfect-fit applications to the step on the Sales Process Map that we're currently considering. That alone makes it a great word. It means something that governs, and it means something that measures. The prospect's objectives govern our overall strategy, and the prospect's objectives are the instrument with which we measure choices in proposal content and style, so that they fit most advantageously.

We spent considerable wordage in Chapter 6, "Qualified Opportunity," on the idea that the key to success in helping our competition out of their account base is to dig a little deeper than the average salesman. No matter how often we encounter "price and service" as the chief preoccupations of our prospects, we are to keep resolutely probing for those concerns that are especially linked to the execution of the prospective customer's business plan. We look for the features of their terrain that most dramatically impact their goals, and we search for ways to link our product or service to those spots. As we gather together after the meeting, considering the best possible ways to keep the transition process rolling on, the prospect's special concerns are where we set our sights.

It's Not About You

Another guiding principle for the preparation and delivery of your proposal: *It's not about how great you are.* Very few of your competitors are ever going to make a presentation that includes, "Essentially we're a bunch of incompetent nincompoops, with no track record. And we're unprincipled too! We're going to promise you great prices and services, then we're going to screw you every chance we get. If you want high costs and poor service, we're your guys!'"

But many of your competitors are going to spend considerable time talking about themselves in a flattering light. In the same way that price and service, as a primary focus, reduces you to an undistinguished commodity-provider, too much emphasis on yourself and your firm in a presentation places you in the Tower of Babble. You don't want to get into a chest-pounding contest in order to win an account. It's very difficult (not to mention sleep-inducing for the prospect) to try and differentiate yourself based upon statements about you or your company's unique strengths. The field of self-proclaimed uniqueness is overcrowded. Anybody can claim anything. There's no differentiation under that rock.

Differentiation lies *way* on the side of imaginative focus on what you've learned about the prospect's special objectives (excluding price and service). The deeper you go into their most essential concerns, the deeper the impression you make. It doesn't even matter if someone at your presentation doesn't immediately remember your name. If given a choice, I'd much rather be known as "that guy who did all the homework and really seems to understand our business" than Tom Redmond. They'll make a point of learning my name soon enough.

The Sales Process Map applies to an extraordinarily wide range of salespeople, in a wide range of sales forces, large and small. Here's a tip for the small. Intensely focused concentration on the customer's unique objectives is the best possible way to overcome any prospect's irrational prejudice in favor of far-larger competitors. It's a proven fact that sales forces from large companies can become complacent, rest too much on their brand, and get outfoxed by diligent, goal-oriented, deep-digging up-and-comers. Who proved it? Most humbly, yours truly. And Joan of Arc. And Galileo.

166

Some significant percent of the people you meet (significant enough to boost you to goal-attainment) are going to be in your corner, rooting for you. Complacency is not an appealing characteristic. It's unappealing enough to give the properly motivated small outfit a fair share of upsets. But that door is only available to you if you find those customer objectives that enable you to develop a differentiated approach.

Who's the Quarterback?

You are. You're the one who targeted the account, developed the contact strategy, made the call, set up the appointment and attended the meeting. You know the prospect's objectives first-hand. It's your job to make sure that those objectives frame all of your follow-up.

And you have another job. You're not only competing with other firms that are pitching for the prospect's business (and it's always advisable to assume that you have plenty of competition, because you do. There's never an advantage in acting as if you have the stage to yourself). But you're also competing for the internal resources of your firm. And that means people. Chapter 6, "Qualified Opportunity," underscored the resources at stake in pursuing new business. You've become a selective salesperson who places a high value on your, and your company's, resources.

Two guys might be able to throw the ball the same distance with the same degree of accuracy. In fact, one might be an altogether better athlete. But somehow the other guy gets across the goal line with greater consistency. Why? Because somehow his teammates can *feel* something intangible coming from him. He's focused, and that focus draws them in and energizes them. They play with an extra something. It's irresistible and unstoppable. It doesn't depend on the weather, or the refs, or the sportswriters, or the fans, or anything. It comes from inside and manifests on the scoreboard.

You're going to put together a team, and *you're* already drawing upon the deepest stuff imaginable: your personal and professional goals. Let people (technical experts, proposal-assemblers, number-crunchers) *feel* the value they bring to you. Bring everybody into your take on the prospect and your assessment of the worthiness of the target. You'll get more than support, you'll get a *push*. Your co-workers will derive energy from participation in a directed, purposeful pursuit.

Your job as project leader is to make sure that your proposal and presentation are soaked in the customer's objectives. But not even the best quarterback calls every play himself. We've mentioned the importance of *listening* in a couple of places. For example, when a gatekeeper picks up your call, or when a prospect is talking. Hold the notion of your extended self close to the surface as you're preparing to follow up on your initial meeting.

Your teammates and management might have some very valuable insight to contribute, and by inviting people to participate in proposal-strategizing and *really listening*, you not only draw upon the widest possible amount of available information, but you make an investment in the future. You're already increasing your personal value by moving step-by-step from goals, through targeting, to the opportunity to make a qualified proposal.

Teamwork is an opportunity to spread your energy and distinguish yourself within the sales force. The rewards of the account-qualification process include making you a salesperson that other people pull for and want to work with, *because they can feel the value you attribute to them*. (And they might not even know that they *really are* a part of your extended self, if they haven't read this book yet. You might suggest that they buy a copy. Or three.) As your value builds, you'll find that people enjoy working with you and that the momentum around your efforts builds and spreads. Another feedback loop.

Building to Team Assembly and Presentation Preparation: the Foundation

There is a wide range of resources available to salespeople in support of the effort to land business. In very large concerns there might be marketing departments, research, financial analysis, writers, graphic artists, and proposal-putter-togetherers all available to assist in the preparation and presentation of materials. Smaller firms might be comparatively limited in their resources. That's where, for example, FedEx/Kinko's comes into play. No matter what your size, you build your team assembly and proposal preparation from the same starting point: customer objectives.

An underlying principle of the Sales Process Map is the notion of *stepping back* before moving on. We initially stepped back to establish our personal and professional goals before moving forward on *anything*. In targeting accounts, we stepped back to get a broad view of who we are as targeting instruments (our individual and extended selves past, present and future). We stepped back to evaluate potential targets. We took a deep look at the implications of qualifying an account. We placed the actual process of making calls within a large framework that resulted in proper-sizing the project and showing it for the very manageable job that it actually is. Now, as you're looking at your next move, it's time to step back again and take a fresh look at the situation. Stepping back invigorates. It makes the old and tired new and lively. It imparts our energy to our output.

So let's first do a little rough sketching on this proposal and presentation business. Before you start gathering people and materials together to advance the transition process in your follow-up with the prospect, take a little time by yourself (or with your sales cohort) and with your #2 pencil and yellow pad. You've already made notes of the prospective customer's objectives. Place them on the table in front of you and get a glass of water or a cup of coffee or tea or a soft drink. Close the door. Get comfortable; put your feet up on a chair. Invoke the muse if you're so inclined. Get loose.

The little exercise we're involved in is a bit of free association. The customer objectives are our focal point. We can take a look at our notes if we need a little prod, but we already have a good grip on them. The point here is to kick back and sketch out a wish list. The list centers on the question, "If we could gather together every resource imaginable to help the prospect in achieving their goals (as related to our product or service), what would we want?"

We think of things from the point of the customer objectives *only*, without regard to the resources we have on hand and which we routinely call upon from our store of in-house capabilities, practices and habits. The idea is to get out of our habitual response patterns and put ourselves in the customer's shoes. It's not about us. If we had access to an infinite supply of resources, what would we choose?

For example, if we were a commercial real estate broker pitching to represent a bank in the development of a remote data center, we might wish (based on prospect objectives) for expertise in:

- construction requirements peculiar to data centers

- security

- electrical supply issues (e.g., amount required, back-up power generation, relative reliability and costs of different utilities)

- local incentive programs

- relative ease of doing business vis-à-vis permitting, zoning

- labor pool: cost, education levels and availability of applicable continuing education, supply, competition, subsidized training

- cost of housing

- demographics

- taxes—property, income and sales

- specialized legal advice in wrapping power supply in appropriate language

- maximum awareness of available sites

- financial analysis in projecting costs of individual components and the overall project, lease vs. purchase

The list could go on. Some of the items on the list might directly respond to specific objectives mentioned by the prospect; for example, they expressed concern about the availability of labor. Other items might be free-associated tangential topics that pop into your mind. What we're asking here is, "If the customer wants to know about available labor in various markets, and I could select from all possible resources to satisfy that concern, what tools would I like to have at my disposal, and what would I like to know?"

Asking that question gives us a new set of eyes. It expands and deepens our response. We'd like to know about housing costs, income taxes, community colleges, subsidized training programs, competition for labor and more. You might say to yourself, "All of that is already included in the idea 'labor pool,' so if I simply bring someone to the presentation who can research her way around demographics and labor statistics, then I won't have to waste time thinking about all that detail. And we have someone like that, right in our marketing department. That's what we're paying her for." You might have someone like that right there in your marketing department, or of course, there's Google™.

But remember, you're the quarterback. Each stated objective of the prospect is surrounded by a constellation of related subgroups. If you say to your marketing director, "I want to have something about labor markets in my presentation," then you're not putting enough energy into the topic. You're entirely invested in wrapping the objectives in as much substantive material as possible.

As a commercial real estate broker, you don't take an objective, "advantageous labor pool," and hand it back to the prospect by saying, "We'll help you land in an advantageous labor pool, and here's the person who's going to do it." That's not going deep enough into the subject. The prospect might not even be aware of what criteria go into labor pool evaluation. Maybe you aren't either. But by taking the time to try and expand on the topic, you'll help your marketing support to head in the direction of a special, differentiated response.

We're not interested in burying the prospect in useless information just to show how smart we are. But we *are* interested in looking at each objective from as many angles as our little free-association exercise will provide. Again, the prospect has concerns other than just "buying stuff and selling stuff," or "insuring stuff," or "moving people from one place to another," or "assembling computer peripherals and then selling them." They have unique underlying niches and challenges that drive their business and with which we're trying to connect. We don't go directly to an objective and say, "We're going to solve that." We step back and try to place the objective in *its* context and to base our proposal and presentation on a more thoroughly imagined, insightful, and practically useful foundation than the prospect's going to get from anyone else.

There's a universal tendency for proposals and presentations to devolve into cookie-cutterness. You've made dozens of pitches, and it's a heck of a lot easier to take an old proposal, plug in references to the prospective customer, then re-utilize boilerplate material to round out the package. The problem with that type of response is that it *feels* tired because it *is* tired. The boilerplate material (your history, your customers, your capabilities, your special features, etc.) tends to veer toward *you*. And to veer toward you in a trite way.

The same goes with presentations. "Bob, remember the presentation we made to Bonzo International? Well, Acme's looking for the same kind of help, and I'd like you to come along and do your thing." Maybe you have a tendency to reuse the same proposal assistors and co-presenters because you're comfortable with them. Or because you enjoy their company. Or because they're funny and great yackers. It's unlikely that the prospect is going to gain territory in their field because you're comfortable with Bob and he's funny, or because you *always* rely on Jim to put together your proposals. (Don't worry. We'll address the situation where you have no choice *but* Bob or Jim.)

The point here is to move completely to the side of customer objectives. Spend some time thinking about other topics that come to mind in connection with those objectives. Don't unconsciously slide into envisioning a proposal or presentation based on resources available to *you*, or habitual response modes from *your* past. That's too limited a mindset. Those past responses have too much *you* in them. They're limited by *your* habits and resources. We've got to try and get out of that rut. The objectives will be our ladder.

Assembling the Team

As you consider the human resources who are going to be deployed in your ongoing transition project, pull your hand back when you find yourself reaching out to someone because you've worked with him or her before in similar situations. Think of the customer objectives and the topics that surround those objectives, the topics you've jotted down in your little free-association exercise.

Step back and try to take a look at personnel with your new set of goal-driven eyes, evaluating them on the basis of their skill sets and experience as they relate to your prospect's objectives. This is an excellent opportunity to expand your view of your own workplace, to take a new look at the capabilities that surround you. You may discover an inclination to look at departments that you have never before considered as resources for sales support.

In talking up your project with a new face from a department that you're rather unfamiliar with, you'll be expanding your sphere of contacts, spreading your energy, finding new information and perhaps new tools. Maybe you've never included someone from your legal department in a presentation, or someone from your IT department. To reiterate, each prospect has unique objectives. The extent to which you approach each proposal opportunity from a focus on those objectives, drawing on every imaginable human resource, is the extent to which you build toward novelty and relevance in your output: proposal and presentation.

You might be saying to yourself, "Listen, Redmond. Get real. We have a certain way of doing proposals in which we're heavily invested, and it's not as if the whole company's available to me to help close a deal." Or, "Listen, Redmond. Get real. We're a small business. We don't *have* an IT department or a legal department or a construction department. We have Jim and Bob. They've been in our business for a long time, and they've seen it all." Those are certainly legitimate observations, but they shouldn't serve to prevent us from taking the widest possible perspective on customer goals and the very best means of hitting those goals.

If we work in a very large organization, we simply won't ever know the limits of our resources unless we do some exploration. Unless we search out every possible way to present a tailored response to a prospect, we'll head right for the "tried and true" without ever knowing how much of the "unique and relevant" we're leaving unexplored. If we work in a small organization, with very limited resources, there's always the possibility of reaching outside, to our law firm or our accountants or one of our suppliers, for expertise that can distinguish our response.

Team building, as a facet of proposal preparation, presents an excellent opportunity to nurture our referral cultivation. Remember your extended self as manifest in the people you've come to know over the years (Chapter 2). Make some calls and seek advice in addressing a challenging requirement presented by the prospect. People are often flattered by being given the opportunity to offer helpful ideas. And, as you're building a referral base, you might find an opportunity for expansion, someone who says, "I don't know much about that area, so I don't see how I can help you. But call so-and-so, and use my name. She might point you in the right direction." While you're at it (and if it's appropriate), you're going to ask these contacts if they have any history with or insight into Acme.

So, maybe at the end of the day, you've taken the widest possible overview of the prospect's objectives and of your available resources. It looks like you're going to rely on the same people you always rely on. It has still been a very worthy exercise. Going through the process has served to instill in all of you a focus on the prospect's objectives. It will turn you more toward the customer's perspective and shake you and your team out of auto-response. Auto-response isn't worthy of your value, Bob and Jim's value, or the prospect's value.

Reconfirm Specifications

You're now somewhere between ankle deep and knee deep in the process of preparing follow-up to your initial appointment. Before you get hip deep, it's time to make a call. We've already talked about this call in the last chapter under "Can We Do Business Together? Take A Sounding." It's to the person with whom you held the first appointment. You told her you'd be following up by phone about a week after the meeting in order to give her a chance to run your discussion and plan of action past all who might be involved in the decision-making chain. If she hasn't had a chance to make the rounds, then give her another week. But by all means, *reconfirm the specifications*. Make sure that you're on the right path, that you're aware of any suggestions or objections that may have arisen.

Building Toward the Proposal and Presentation

Each time we set about addressing solutions to a new prospect's needs, we start by taking all of the proposals we've done in the past and leaving them right where they are, in the files. In "Assembling the Team" we've used the objectives as a launching pad for expanding our perspective on the prospect's objectives and environment, for finding tangential, perhaps no-so-obvious, useful subheadings that will ultimately serve to frame a fresh take on a specialized delivery of our goods or services. We've built the team upon these objectives. Even if we end up working with familiar faces, we've invited them into our point of view and reset their sights on a unique response. We might even have reached outside our firm for special expertise, if such an arrangement is practicable.

When setting up to develop our proposal, we then find that we've already gathered a pile of fresh material with which to build our content. The widest possible net of ideas was cast when we kicked back and imagined *everything and everybody* that we might wish to have at our disposal in satisfying the prospect's objectives. During team assembly, this wish list was transformed into deliverables as dictated by the resources actually available to us. Now we can take those deliverables and arrange them into a tailored proposal of solutions. The proposal must include:

1. A restatement of the prospect's objectives

2. Your program for attaining the objectives. This is your opportunity to demonstrate the depth and novelty that you bring to the table. Don't include every idea that crosses your mind—only those ideas which have valid bearing on the objectives, or those ideas, while not obvious, which you believe will bring strong support to the program and, possibly, shed more light on the objectives than the prospect could have envisioned. Take a chance. If you really believe that investment in a new forklift would be a waste of money if the warehouse floor isn't resurfaced, then say it. If you believe that the prospect is predisposed to spend unnecessary money, then say so. We'll expand on this area in the next chapter, "Presentation—Going Live."

3. Team—Names and specialties as they relate to your program, no major biographies

4. Price or framework for establishing price (expanded in the next chapter)

5. Transition:

  - Steps (for example, how to achieve seamless replacement of existing vendor)

  - Timetable (when and what to expect as milestones on the road to you)

6. Expectations:

  - What the prospect can expect in terms of results

  - How the success of your program will be measured

We're strong believers in "less is more." Your written proposal (hardcopy, PowerPoint, DVD—it's the customer's call) should stay as close to bullet points as possible. The presumption here is that the written material is prelude or accompaniment to a face-to-face presentation. Decision-makers are more likely to be impressed by "lean and meaningful" than by bulk. That's why they call them decision-makers. That's all we're going to say about the proposal and presentation for now. See you next chapter.

We entirely forgot to mention your magnificent history. And your great personality. Oops! We'll get to it.

(Your Name), Inc. Sales Process

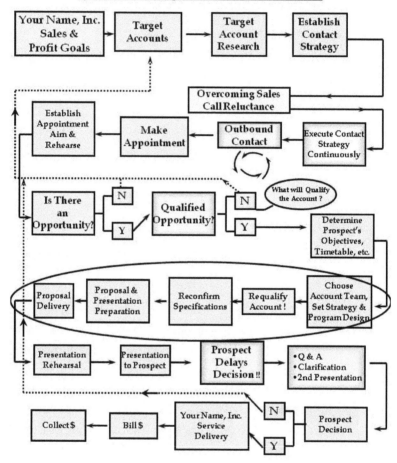

Copyright©Redmond Group, Inc. 2011

Chapter 9

PRESENTATION
Going Live

Radical Notion #4: Rehearsal is the foundation for the drafting of your proposal, and for the highest-impact, freshest live delivery of what it is you have to say in that proposal. It has priority status #1. It's the wellspring from which all else will follow. How's that for a radical notion—rehearsing first, *then* writing the proposal, and finally preparing for the live presentation? (Note to reader: Scanning for Radical Notions #1, 2 and 3 is guaranteed to produce the side-benefit of reanimating your take on previous and upcoming material.)

The Conservation of Energy: Garden-Fresh Delivery to the Prospect

We're going live with our proposal and presentation to the prospect. It would be a shame to lose any of the novelty and substance that's been gathered up to this point. And it's easy to do! Most salespeople do it all of the time. We lose that novelty and substance by taking the customer objectives and sitting *right* down to draft a proposal that will serve as the basis of the presentation and handing it to your teammates as a finished script. Worse yet is taking the objectives and handing them off to a staff proposal-writer and saying, "Here are the prospect's objectives, see what you can come up with." A lot goes down the drain with this approach.

Let's measure what's lost: We took a wide perspective in gathering a rich group of prospects, we spent considerable energy in making contact and securing an appointment or a series of appointments, we focused on the prospect's differentiating characteristics, we built a deep and substantial appreciation of customer objectives, and we put together the most responsive team possible. We lose all of that richness if we're careless about final payload delivery. Our chances of getting the order move close to the same odds as those of the competition. As we said before, we're not in this to end up with a lottery ticket; that's a losing strategy. This is just not acceptable.

Our team is the human form of the goal-shaped and differentiated approach we've gleaned from the Sales Process Map. They're the living embodiment of all that's brought us to this point. And they have ideas! That's why they're on the team. And they can talk (or communicate in some other mode). They'll be participating at the presentation. It's huddle time. Gather 'em together. Some might be online virtual attendees, but all must attend.

We're not talking about a brainstorming session here. We've done enough brainstorming in getting to this point. We're talking about homing in on proposal development and presentation delivery. The difference is that now we're narrowing our focus to the vibrant originality we've already fostered, an originality rooted in our goals. It's what sets us apart from the horde.

Framework for Rehearsal—Proposal Essentials

We introduced the proposal essentials at the end of the last chapter. It's a simple structure, covering the following:

- Statement of customer objectives
- Your program for attaining the objectives
- Introduction of your team
- Pricing
- Transition from the current supplier to you
- Expectations

This first rehearsal is where we put flesh on these essentials. It's where we gather the spontaneity and personal involvement that will supply the content and shape the delivery of the presentation.

Statement of Customer Objectives

Bring some sort of recording device to the meeting. Turn it on. Bring a mega-pad, mounted on an easel, and a magic marker, or use a white board, or better yet, an electronic board where you can send your notes out via e-mail and print hard copies. Then ask the group for a statement of customer objectives. Warned you that this was radical.

Of course, *you* already know the objectives. You've mulled them over and looked at them from all angles. You've already brainstormed ancillary topics that surround the objectives that bring them into greater relief and provide unique avenues for accessing objective achievement. (See Chapter 8, "How to Get an Order, Part II: A Building Project: Building a Team, Building Toward a Proposal and Presentation.")

In assembling the team, you, the point person, have already prepped your colleagues on the basics of the opportunity that you're pursuing together. Don't start off with what *you* already know. Let people try to put into words what they think the customer is after. They can even say "good prices and great service" with impunity. Perhaps they'll say something that sparks a new train of thought. Perhaps they'll display an acute lack of understanding about your attempt to attach the proposal to unique characteristics of the prospect. No problem. You can iron out those issues later.

The only thing that's intolerable is a pronounced lack of interest in the rehearsal. In such a case, pull the teammate aside at the end and find out if it's a "bad day" issue, or if he or she is constitutionally resistant to your way of getting an order. When you first broached the project, he might have been gung-ho, but now that you're actually rehearsing your way to presentation, he might have concluded that you've overdosed on Redmond. That's not OK. We're not advocating "sales team as cult" here; individuality is a plus. But neither are we looking to embed resistors in the presentation. We don't need any energy leaks; our goal is a lively, substantive, value-packed presence.

As teammates give their ideas on the prospect's objectives, jot them down on the mega pad with magic marker for everyone to see. This process shouldn't take long, but it's important for several reasons. It provides you with a measure of your group's initial orientation to the target. You'll get some feedback that's dead-on, and you'll get some that's totally off the mark. No matter. You're trying to establish the base from which you'll guide your team toward the presentation version of the objectives. Getting everyone's input, right or wrong, helps build cohesiveness within the team and makes everyone a participant in constructing the proposal. Again, it's not impossible that a new insight will arise.

After the teammate input, it's your turn to start to shape the discussion around *your* take on customer objectives. (After all, *you* get a turn too!) You haven't simply stood in front of the room and dictated the program. You've already started a give-and-take, *a participatory process that recognizes the value of your colleagues*. This is your opportunity to highlight and drive home those unique characteristics of the prospect that will enable you to end up with a special presentation. This rehearsal is the mechanism that insures, from the very start, that everyone is on board. It instills a sense of purpose, direction and integration. Everyone will know his or her assignment, and everyone will see the same goal line.

This is where you reinforce to your colleagues your overview on supporting the business of your prospective account. This is where you take an objective—"more butts in the seats" for a bus company—and connect it to a comprehensive safety inspection program (low insurance premiums don't suffice; safety works for everybody and can become identified with the brand). This is where you take "low-cost data processing" and tie it to available housing and employee continuing education opportunities (initial low occupancy and operating costs don't suffice; you're concerned about long-time stability of the labor market in the recommended locale).

> One more time. What are the objectives of the prospect? We promise this—after you ask this question twice, it will become totally natural for you.

On *your* turn to comment on objectives, you can instill a sense that you're going to move the ball across the goal line together, that the homework's already done:

- You understand the competitive terrain from the customer's point of view

- You've expanded on the originally stated objectives to uncover those topics that will serve the purposes of goal achievement, and which the prospect hadn't yet considered

- You've mustered a team that is as capable as possible of bringing in the business. "Thanks for joining me!"

Where the team's input has been on the mark, circle it on your mega pad. Then jot down the additional topics which you believe should be included. And make it clear that deep service is the team's goal, deep service as evidenced by your extra-mile "care and feeding" of customer objectives. The electricity will spread through the room.

When you emerged from your initial meeting(s) with the prospect, you carried out with you a set of objectives. You followed up to confirm those objectives, to make sure that you were heading in the right direction and to determine if there were any suggestions or objections to the path chosen by you and by the prospect's team of people with whom you had met. Back in the office you brainstormed those objectives and perhaps uncovered topics that would bring strong support to goal achievement. These topics serve, incidentally, to differentiate your response.

But, as we're listing customer objectives, we highlight those objectives that are precisely in the language that emerged way back from our initial meeting and our subsequent reconfirmations. Those are our major headings under *Objectives*. Those topics that *we've* turned up, and that we feel *truly* shed light on the achievement of primary objectives, fit *under* the appropriate major objective as subheadings. We believe in always bringing our imagination and experience to bear in expanding the scope of objectives. But we don't believe in allowing our imagination to overwhelm the customer's own perspective on their own issues. We introduce subjects outside of those stated by the customer with the clear indication that, in our belief, they are areas that should be investigated to reach the highest quality solution to a stated objective.

Your Program for Attaining the Objectives

This procedure is going to save you (or someone on your staff) a lot of time and energy spent on creative writing. The component parts of the proposal are going to naturally emerge from this rehearsal. It's going to emerge in a succinct and "bullet point" form. It will be fresh, with an intrinsic spontaneity. And it will be hardwired to the presentation since it arises from a team effort, not from a single-handed summarization of objectives and proposed solutions.

Some businesses never spend a lot of time and energy on creative writing. There is a tendency on the part of many sales organizations to "automate" proposal and presentation development. The idea is to develop a "stock" format and even "stock" content, then to add items that will give the appearance of a "fit" for a particular prospect. We suppose it's a time-saving strategy, the idea being, "Why should we start from scratch? We've done dozens of pitches. Let's have a template that we can just modify." The trouble with such a prescription is that it's fatigued by its very nature. And that fatigue will show, especially when compared with your competition, which has purchased several copies of *Selling From the Inside Out* and actually read and implemented what it has to say.

What we're proposing is the exact opposite: *all* uniquely relevant content, and *perhaps* some "stock," but not much. For example, you don't have to come up with totally original, custom-fit names for yourselves. It might be going a bit overboard to invent special new names for each person on the team depending on the needs of the customer, like "Safety Man" or "Distribution Chain Woman." Jim, Joan, or Alice will do, with last names.

In order to achieve our personal and professional goals, we need to book business from prospects whose characteristics will get us to those goals. The idea of "saving time" by relying on rehashed materials doesn't jibe with a high probability of transitioning accounts to us. Additionally, it really doesn't take more energy to produce a standout, useful proposal; it falls out naturally from this rehearsal. When it comes to presentation, we believe that it's more difficult for even the best salesman to overcome tired material than it is to deliver something that's alive with relevance and originality. "Stock" material is, by definition, about the presenter, not about the prospect.

Wedging customer objectives into a fixed template means that you're placing your convenience over the prospect's needs. It will show, and show to your disadvantage. Don't forget, the people to whom you're making your presentation have been on the other side of the table. They can smell re-worked material from a mile off. The essential components of the proposal that we're suggesting aren't the same thing as "stock" content. The "essentials" are only a framework, meant to be dominated by content.

Some wise old philosopher (we're pretty sure it was Lao Tse) said that the most effective leader is the one who leaves those under his command with the feeling that they did everything by themselves. (That must assume that things worked out well.) It's a worthy principle to apply to proposal development. Think of yourself as a guiding spirit and not as a fearsome general when moving on to the solutions for the objectives that you've just listed.

Having finished your list under *Objectives*, it's time to start another list, *Solutions*. Let's remember, the team that's sitting around the room represents all of the energy you've expended in finding the best possible solutions to customer objectives. (See previous chapter, subheadings "Building to Team Assembly and Presentation Preparation—The Foundation" and "Assembling the Team.") Run down the list of objectives and direct yourself to the team member who will have responsibility for handling a given topic. Remember that the *major* headings are the objectives as articulated and confirmed by the prospect.

We're not envisioning this from scratch. In putting the team together, you've already had the opportunity to address each member individually, to brief him or her on the opportunity at hand, and to outline how you feel that his or her particular skills and experience can bring real value in transitioning the account to your outfit.

Let the team member state the proposed solution in her own terms. As with the summation of *Objectives*, we aim to instill a participatory element in our preparation. This will result in a strong, animated, engaging presentation. Your team will represent ideas which they have had a hand in developing, ideas that have arisen from a recognition of *their* value. We don't hand a fully worked-out script to a teammate; we *develop* a script cooperatively. After all, each person is on the team because he or she has something substantive to offer. The way to bring that substance to the surface with the greatest amount of vitality is to start from *her* perspective on the solution.

Your job in the rehearsal is to make sure that the objectives are always at center stage. As a teammate sets out on an elaboration of the solution under her sphere of authority, first *listen*, then *guide*. There are many things you might learn. You might learn that she has a better grasp on the situation than *you* do. You might learn that she doesn't have a clear idea of her role and what you expect of her.

All of this is useful stuff. You might think to yourself, "Holy mackerel! What a dynamo. I think I'll make *her* the M.C. and take a support role for myself." On the other hand, if she seems uncertain about the solution that she represents, it may be because she doesn't clearly understand the objective, or because both of you haven't sufficiently worked out and clarified the solution you expect her to champion.

This is where the beauty of serious rehearsal shines through. As you listen to your teammates, you'll learn how far you have to go to get things tightly bound to the objectives. Since everybody is in one room, they'll *all* be learning as you *guide* each initial statement on solutions toward the most "objective-focused" form. All of the give-and-take that takes place will serve not only to make sure that each particular solution is presented in the clearest possible light, but to drive home (again and again) your vision of what it will take to produce the desired end product—a lean, focused, fresh, irresistible invitation for the prospect to transition to your book of accounts.

Each member of the team who has responsibility for handling a specific *major* objective takes a turn at voicing the solution. Then through dialogue with you (the guardian of the objectives), a finely honed, brief restatement of the solution is worked out and jotted down. *Everybody's* learning during this process. Where you've expanded on a topic (suggesting perhaps that the potential purchaser of your new fuel-efficient forklift should re-surface the warehouse floor and get new lighting while they're at it), you go through the same process. This expansion might be handled by someone different than the custodian of the *major* objective under which it is located.

We hear the voices. "Redmond, you're cracked! We don't have an unlimited supply of experts to bring to every presentation. Get real." It doesn't matter whether you can address each solution with a specialist of some sort. The team you've assembled is the best grouping you can put together given your resources. The important thing is to *rehearse first,* using the essentials as a guideline. In the case where you're going to end up giving the presentation alongside the same three familiars with whom you always work, you will still be reorienting them and yourself toward a strictly objective-focused mindset and clearly stated solutions. Even if you're a one-man show, *rehearse first.* It's where all proposal content and presentations are born.

Introduction of Your Team

The hard copy (or DVD or PowerPoint) version of the proposal will have an entry for the names of your teammates. But there is no "stock" biographical information after the name. The short descriptive material that follows the name of each participant should include *very* brief statements of special skills and experience related specifically to their role on the team.

As a practical matter, each member of the team will be introduced by you at the outset of the meeting. It's our belief that when it's time for a team member to address the solution to an objective, it's best for them to dive right into the matter with no elaboration on their personal biography. Biographical material is available in the hard copy, as suggested in the previous paragraph. Customer interest in your biographies is most valuable if it arises naturally from the fact that the prospect is impressed by your focused concentration on imaginative solutions to clearly understood objectives. If they want to know more about you after the presentation, it's most likely because you've aroused their interest. There's always plenty of time after the presentation to tell them more about you; there isn't always plenty of time to tell them more about your program of solutions.

Pricing

People like to know how much things are going to cost, and we don't believe in leaving the issue of price as bait for "further discussion." That's an irritating ploy in the eyes of most prospective buyers. Give the prospect a pricing structure based upon *all* of the product and service to be provided by *you* under your full program of solutions. Don't include recommended responses that will be fulfilled by others. You're not going to be the one who resurfaces the warehouse floor no matter how much it needs to be done.

Remember, your program may well include items that are beyond the scope of what the customer *thought* they needed in order to achieve their objectives. But you have presented *all* that you believe should be done in order for them to arrive at the very best, highest impact solution. Quality and thoroughness have been your guides. Don't be afraid that you're going to go beyond their budget expectations and frighten them away.

A thoroughly prepared menu of solutions to correctly understood objectives puts price where it belongs: subservient to substance. You've developed a comprehensive approach to issues that are facing your prospect. You've taken the time and energy to view the objectives in such a way that *everything* which affects their successful achievement is considered. Your pricing should reflect *all* of the input. Let the chips fall where they may. You want follow-up on pricing to be immersed in discussion of the objectives and the best possible program of solutions, not on "everyday low prices."

Maybe the prospect has some different ideas than those presented in your program. That's OK. As long as the back-and-forth stays focused on the substance of your proposal, then the objectives are center stage, where they belong. A pricing structure should fall naturally from the most comprehensive approach to solutions. No qualified account is going to run away because of an initial price proposal. If you've been following the Sales Process Map, you'll find that reaction to your approach stays focused on the meat of the matter: achievement of customer objectives. Pricing will humbly follow, as it should.

Presentation

Transition from the Current Supplier to You

In Chapter 7, "How to Get an Order, Part I," we discussed the notion of maintaining the visibility of *transition to you* as a constant drumbeat during the *entire* sales process. It has followed us into the rehearsal, and it will continue to follow us all the way to the actual transition. Throw the topic of transition out for open discussion between yourself and your colleagues. The idea here is to highlight all of the steps, procedures, critical junctures, scheduling issues, paperwork and responsibilities (yours and the customer's) that will need to be carefully managed in transitioning the business from the current supplier to you.

"Wait a minute, Redmond! Isn't it just a little too pushy and presumptuous to spend a prospect's time, in a live presentation, on the issue of transition, when you don't even have any feedback on their total response to your program? Get real." We'll grant you a quarter of a nod on that observation. But only a quarter. Most of the presentation will be spent on your program of solutions. However, don't forget, we're on a path to transition. A short, "lean and meaningful" review of transition items in the rehearsal will emerge as powerful and differentiated content in the presentation.

Examining all of the issues (scheduling, approvals and procedures) that surround transition also serves to tighten up your entire program. Each member of the team should be able to state, with respect to her sphere of responsibility, how a seamless move from the current supplier to you is to be achieved. Enumerating all of the steps that are required to shepherd the account through the transition requires that you really take a deep look at your program, and that you open up a substantive look at how the prospect manages those segments of their business that will be directly impacted by the switch to you. A substantial and thorough address of the customer's objectives is the core of your presentation. Including transition, however, will demonstrate just how all-encompassing is the overview that you bring to the table. There's also the not-so-subtle message that you're using to relieve the competition of the burden of their business.

Reminder: Don't overlook the sample Transition Chart on our website, where you can freely edit and modify the chart to best reflect your prospect's circumstances, necessary tasks and timetable.

Expectations

The final stage of rehearsal, the acid test—can your teammates (briefly) articulate what the prospect should expect as the result of the implementation of your program? The whole production is built upon customer objectives. Each team member should state, with specificity, how his particular area of the solution ties back to the objectives. It's not good enough to say, "You'll have more comprehensive coverage." The recommendations you've made need to be reinforced as leading, in a fundamental way, back to the objectives. We've tried to go beyond the obvious, price and good service, in our understanding of the objectives. If we've succeeded in linking our program to deep operational characteristics of the prospect's business, then we should be able to demonstrate *how* our proposals will work out on the playing field.

Our goals (way back in Chapter 1) had three "must" features. They were *meaningful, measurable*, and *written*. Let each teammate propose a method of measuring the effectiveness and impact of his recommendations: "When we take this step, you will see this result, which will boost distribution efficiency in the range of this percent." You're not just selling; you're out to increase value. Take a stab at proposing a measure of that value.

Hardcopy: The Rehearsal in Words

The rehearsal's over; your colleagues can go back to their workstations. You can turn off the recording device. The hardcopy proposal that's going to accompany your presentation (in whichever format the prospect prefers) is going to be extracted, by you, directly from your mega-pad notes.

There's no need for you or any staff writer to invoke the muse and settle into an arduous creative writing exercise. And there's certainly no need to recycle old material. Your job is simply to organize and state, as briefly as possible, all of the nuggets that dropped out naturally from the rehearsal. They are to be organized under the simple concepts from which they were generated: statement of objectives, program for attaining objectives, team, pricing, transition, expectations. Remember, everything's to be stated in short bullet-point form—no enlightened elaboration. The idea is to respect the value of your prospect's time and intelligence, and besides, you're going to be making a presentation. During and after the presentation there will be give-and-take; plenty of time for expansion, if necessary.

Your job as editor is simply to preserve the guided development of content that emerged from the rehearsal and which contains all of the spontaneity and focus of the entire Sales Process Map. There is to be no concern with "beefing up" the hard copy in order to achieve some sort of dramatic impact from the thickness of the proposal. Your proposal will stand out because of its clarity, usefulness, and focus.

We're not schoolkids trying figure out how to get more pages into a report, and we're not trying to convince someone that they should hire us because we've worked for such-and-such corporation in the past. An audience can instinctively tell the difference between reliance on "tried and true" habits of presentation, and effort that concerns itself strictly and imaginatively with a clear program built upon a deep understanding of objectives. Let the content fall where it may; all unnecessary embellishment only serves to diminish the impact that you've been so careful to achieve.

We're believers in substance over form. You might even consider removing the "essentials" of the framework (objectives, program, team, etc.) as headings in the final written material. Now that the framework has done its work, let the content speak for itself. After all, you'll be there to guide it.

If you can't figure out something that you've scribbled on the pad, then use your recording device to go back and clear up the issue, or to revisit a discussion that you recall as being particularly interesting and useful. That recording device is a handy tool for support.

When the proposal is drafted, send it around to all teammates for their review and comment. Let them make whatever comments they want. But only those which directly serve the usefulness of your program are of interest.

Once everyone has had a chance to review and comment upon the material, it's time for a final "sound check." Gather everyone together again for a run-through of the final proposal. Everyone has had a hand in developing the parts of the program that fall under his or her role, so there should be nothing new here. Deliver the *entire* presentation as if it were in front of an audience. This produces several important benefits: it further "hardwires" the material into each presenter, it points out redundancies or transitional gaps between topics, and it underscores the professional attitude which binds the group.

Showtime

We're not great adherents to the notion that significant attention must be paid to the protocol and staging of presentations. You've worked hard to produce a substantial program. It's our belief that, just as content overwhelms framework "essentials" in the hardcopy, your living embodiment of solutions should overwhelm concern about seating arrangements, lighting, gadgetry (only what it takes to deliver in the format preferred by the customer), warm-up speeches and such. You're the folks with the answers. Your audience has seen examples of every surefire presentation recommendation available at the bookstores. We're wary of the danger that staging concerns can outshine content and drain energy from your solution-packed presence.

We suppose you could call us "minimalists with a vengeance." There will be plenty of give-and-take in the room. We believe that all energy should be available to this guided dialogue, with none spent on diversions like who sits next to whom, or fidgeting with pins on name tags, or delivering jokey warm-up routines.

Your role as master of ceremonies is simple. You first run down the list of customer objectives. You've verified them already, and you've included on the list as subheadings those additional strategies which you believe will be supportive in the achievement of the primary goals. Let's assume, for the sake of simplicity, that you've made a PowerPoint version of the proposal. The first "slide" will be your brief, bullet-point summary of all those objectives, simply recapped by you.

Then you introduce that member of the team who will have responsibility for directing the solution of a particular objective. She should be backed up by a display or bound hardcopy, *if that's what the customer wants,* that includes a restatement of the objectives and a brief (bullet-point) statement of that part of the solution for which she will be responsible. Her job is to explain the thinking behind your recommendation of that particular approach and the steps that will be followed in its achievement.

In presenting a colleague, there is no need to provide a lengthy, flowery introduction. Let her evident familiarity with the material speak for itself. Remember, there is a summary of the expertise and experience of each of your teammates on the *Team* page. Any expansion required by the customer will come out during the discussion that follows your presentation.

Again, your role as MC is to *guide.* As each colleague covers his particular facet of the solution, there may be a small amount of clarification requested by an audience member. But you've got to keep things moving in order to cover *all* of the objectives. When you see a clarification moving in the direction of a major digression, it's your job to step in and say, "Let's cover that in the Q&A after the full presentation." (And make a note to insure that you *do* cover it.) Your guidance is anchored in full coverage of the objectives, solutions, pricing, transition, and expectations.

By the way, it takes some skill to be a good MC. You have to be able to cut off digressions without letting an audience member feel offended. You have to be able to resist the temptation to keep the air filled with words. For example, when there's silence during pauses, you might have a nervous impulse to throw in some idle banter. Resist that impulse. Silence might indicate thoughtfulness about your program—that's a good thing. Keep in mind all of the substance that your presence embodies. Feel the confidence that arises from your preparation. Don't worry about the scowl that some guy seems to be throwing your way; it's way more likely to be a permanent fixture of his face than it is to be about anything you're saying. Remember, it's not about *you*. It's about achieving objectives.

The solutions are to be presented by each appropriate team member as they arise on the list of objectives. And you, of course, might be wearing two hats, MC and caretaker of a specific solution. When it comes to pricing, transition and expectations, it's better that they be covered by one person (you), with some help from the floor if necessary. Specialized focus is reserved for solutions.

When the presentation is complete, throw the floor open for Q&A. Here your job as guide is reduced to directing queries to the appropriate team member in cases where the questioner doesn't direct it himself. Stick to the solutions. Don't oversell or *ever* allow defensiveness about a specific approach or about pricing to enter the give-and-take. You're not looking for an instant "buy" to come out of this presentation. You're looking for some additional discussion and clarification. But it's not unguided follow-up. It's now more narrowly focused on transition. Come what may.

The Close

Warning—controversy is in this neighborhood! We do not like and have never liked the phrase "closing the sale." But hey, it's so deeply imbedded in our collective sales culture that we'll save that battle for another day and another workshop. Here's our take on closing (write this down): "You are either moving towards a close or away from a close *at all times*." And if you're standing still, you are moving away.

The Sales Process Map is designed so that *every* action and *every* activity is aimed at moving you toward the close. It may bear repeating here—from the third paragraph of this chapter (oh no, now Redmond is quoting Redmond!). Here's what you've done in moving the prospect towards the close: "We took a wide perspective in gathering a rich group of prospects, we spent considerable energy in making contact and securing an appointment or a series of appointments, we focused on the prospect's differentiating characteristics, we built a deep and substantial appreciation of customer objectives, and we put together the most responsive team possible." Every step has the same objective—moving the prospect to the status of client. How can you be denied?

(Your Name), Inc. Sales Process

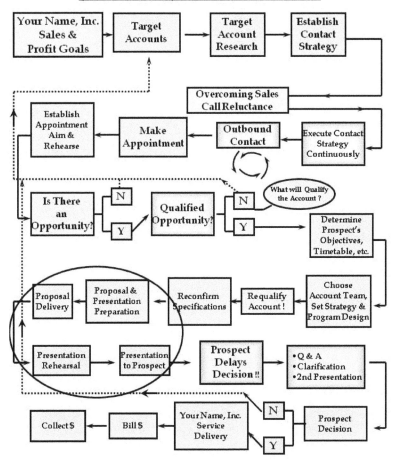

Copyright©Redmond Group, Inc. 2011

Chapter 10

PROSPECT DELAYS THEIR DECISION
Only 100% of the Time

Prospects will delay their decision only 100% of the time—a natural law? It's on the Sales Process Map. It's always been there, and we even laminate these exhibits. This fact has not changed.

I must admit, this is the biggest psychological challenge for me as a professional salesperson. I really wish things were different, but in my experience, the sales process gets stalled for a variety of reasons. How about the biggest one—the FEAR factor? Your prospect's:

- Fear of change

- Desire to avoid the risk inherent in buying from you

- Fear that something may go wrong for them and they will be subjected to criticism

- ROI expectation

- Are you really the solution?

- Can you really help achieve our objectives?

- Trust in you and your team

- Fear about you delivering the goods

We've all heard the following from time to time:

"We're not *that* dissatisfied with our current arrangements."
"We need to think about it."
"The timing is just not right."

To overcome the fear, we've been suggesting a somewhat radical approach—at least some have told us it is radical. Well, here goes:

Radical Notion #3—this notion is so radical that it appears after Radical Notion #4. **Tell the prospect that they are going to delay the decision.** You can sometimes even add, "and don't let us down!" Follow this up with, "Here is a list of the Top Ten reasons why customers do business with us." Note from Redmond: Please have fourteen reasons listed and add, "We couldn't stop at ten!" (And here's the radical part): "Here are the four reasons why you could not do business with our firm."

That's right, name the reasons—this is really where their fear resides.

An example may be helpful. In our own case, we're a small company and, although many times unspoken, there are usually underlying fears like, Can Tom Redmond handle the demands of a large assignment? What if something goes wrong? My nine bosses are going to ask who we used. How do I answer, "Why didn't we use a company like Global Unlimited Powerhouse International with 500 offices around the globe?"

Our solution to diminish, eliminate or outright overcome their fear is that we:

1. Name their fears, say them out loud, and put them in writing.

2. Line the fears up one at a time and either toss them back to hell from where they came or offer a reasonable response.

3. Offer assurances from a third party (like a happy customer or two who have had the identical fears).

4. Keep their eye on the target by reinforcing the objectives that will be achieved by hiring you.

5. Offer to instruct the prospect on how the transition will be made—what happens and when. A spreadsheet showing

critical activities and timing can be a very powerful instructional tool.

Some additional thoughts:

- If this approach is too radical for you, is contrary to everything you feel about the proper way to make a sale, and your internal dialogue is saying "This is nonsense"—drop this concept immediately (but please keep reading).

- As we've stated earlier, your sales process never stands still. You are either moving towards a close or away from a close at all times. Is your prospect's aversion to risk (FEAR) in the way?

- Prospects have many terrific skills, but hiring you is *not* one of them. Why is this so? Here's one thought: How often does your prospect make a change like the one you are proposing? Every three years, five years, ten years, never? Logic dictates that, as a general rule, the prospect does not typically have enough experience to easily and readily make these hiring and firing decisions.

- Early in the sales process, make an agreement with your prospect and explain what actions you plan to take if (make that when) their decision is delayed. For example, you will be free to contact them often. Dialogue kind of like this: "I'll contact you every day until you say 'yes.' " This is the *Green Eggs and Ham* approach. That's right, Dr. Seuss's book of sales—the *second* most effective sales book on the planet. Each subsequent contact helps you to determine what is causing the delay, the root cause of their fear, and enables you to formulate a response to the buyer's objections and manage their risk as you continue to move towards a close.

Q. (From sales professional calling a few days after the proposal was delivered and presented): "Just calling to check in about our proposal and how the decision-making process is going."

A. (From the prospect in the process of delaying): "Thanks for calling, but we're still delaying."

Response from sales professional: "You're doing great."

One week later (same thing).

One week later (same thing).

One week later—Response from sales professional: "Time's up. Let's move forward with your commitment."

(Your Name), Inc. Sales Process

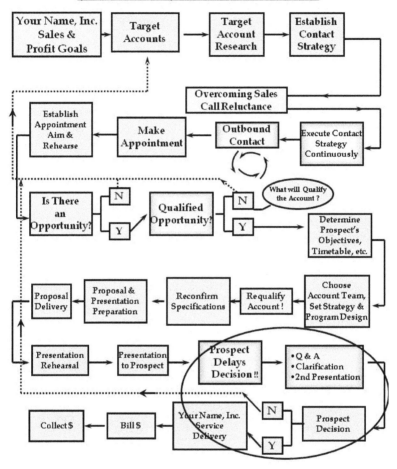

Copyright ©Redmond Group, Inc. 2011

Chapter 11

THE JOURNAL OF FUNK
Fear, Doubt, Despair
(and That's on a Great Day!)

Yes, we know how you feel—you may have actually turned to this chapter first. While planning and designing this book, I wanted to actually use as the title *Fear, Doubt and Despair (and That's on a Great Day)*. Alas, the publisher thought better of this, but happily did agree that we could include a chapter on this important aspect of the sales process, *your* sales process. If you have not experienced fear, doubt and despair in the sales business, don't worry, you will.

Sales professionals at all levels of experience and development encounter fear, doubt, and despair. Perhaps "despair" is a bit over the top. OK then, stick with the fear and doubt part. More on despair later. So how about a proven technique to crush these unwanted, energy-draining intruders and send them back to hell where they came from? You may be thinking that it's time for Tom to switch to decaf.

Here we go again. Take out your high-tech tools—yellow pad and #2 pencil—and simply write down all of these negative intruders without edits; work from the point of view that not a soul will ever read your Journal of Funk. We guarantee that as you execute this task, those intruders will dissolve. Well, at least they will have less power over you.

I'm uncertain where I learned this technique—maybe intuitive, maybe a gift from beyond—but I absolutely assure you that it works. Uh oh, watch out for our old friend resistance. I can hear some of you saying, "What a crock, this will never work!" Now it's time to negotiate with your resistance. Put it on the side; you can pick it up later. Just give this a try. Have I ever let you down before?

Where do these intruders and this internal dialogue come from? The quick answer is that they come from us, or maybe through us. Without too much philosophizing, who cares where they come from? They just appear—with a trigger, without a trigger, who cares? It can, however, be debilitating. It can stop us from moving energetically toward achievement of our goals. For example, how many times have I stopped writing this book? Fear and doubt (for some reason, not much in the despair area).

So how do you react as you awaken to another day and your internal voice says:

- "How's the world gonna screw me today?"

- "Good morning, Tom, today's the day that you will be found out for the loser you are."

- "Good morning, Tom, today's the day when you finally learn that your strategies, your time tested techniques, really aren't worth the powder to send them to hell (and you will be found out for the loser you are)."

- "I'm failing, I have to go to Plan B—I better get a traditional job!"

Some examples of my Journal of Funk entries might be helpful. Of course, I made some edits because when I wrote them up, I wrote as if no one would ever read these. Incidentally, I have a file full of these writings on my desk. They will eventually be found when I am no longer able to get to my desk, but I digress. Here goes:

January 22—Caribou Coffee Shop, Owings Mills, MD
Feeling like crap, low self esteem, great doubt, not so much worry, just a general feeling of down.

Need to crack this open soon or I'll be consumed by it. Maybe pushing my business too hard? , Maybe pushing myself too hard?"

(and it gets better)—lost my way, lost my dream.

OK, Tom, take some action—right now let this go.

February 2

On the way to a business gig:

Today's fear:

- Just general fear
- What if they don't like me?
- What if I make a mistake?
- What do they want?

OK, Tom, you know this fear. Absorb it all, let it wash over you. This meditation is for my healing. Now instead, invite in prosperity, joy, trust, relationships, love—keep breathing in and out, in and out. Take a good look at what you have accomplished. Let the universe provide for you today.

December 11

Feeling the squeeze.

Just feeling the squeeze on several fronts. I think a lot of it has to do with small thinking. Thinking in terms of limitations, not only lack of opportunities but also in terms of something shrinking. Is it the economy? Speaking of shrinkage, how about our pension plan mutual fund losses! Is it the general negativity, anxiety?... and I can't seem to see past it—stuck in a kind of failure mode.

Oh yeah, plus I see nothing but threats to the business. Am I keeping up? Have I run the course? Am I taken seriously? Is it the time of year? The December darkness? Seasonal anxiety disorder—need to check that out—maybe I'm on to something here—fatigue, low level depression—how about a solution?

Oh, I almost forgot about the credit crunch—will we be able to renew our company credit lines? What are we about to face with the approval process?

Also worried about our grown children and I think they are worried about us (hey, that's helpful!). We need to be there for them—can we do it? Do I want to do it? Do they want us to do it?

Something else, I've not been getting enough exercise, feeling criticisms from clients, and while I'm at it, I think I'll drop my spiritual practices as well, they're obviously not working and at least the weather report says that it's going to rain for a few days in a row. Wow, this sounds like a depression to me.

So take some action—let go for today. Trust the process—yes, that's it, I don't trust the process, I don't trust that I'll be OK.

This is very good work, Tom.

I could go on for pages, but you get the idea. The most difficult part of this process is sitting down and doing it. I can assure you—no, I promise you that the process works. Sit down, take out those high-tech devices that we're so fond of (yellow pad and pencil) and begin writing. If you need to put a timer on, go ahead—this can also be helpful. The point is to clear this rubbish out. Don't worry, it will return—so you get to rinse and repeat.

Q. What do you do when in despair?

A. When in despair, despair with enthusiasm. It makes it go away faster.

AFTERWORD
Life from a New Angle

So, over fifteen years ago, your author took a great leap. How has the Sales Process Map and personal and professional goal setting worked out? It's certainly worked out well for my customers, my family (a grandchild flew in along the way), and so, for me. You may be asking what direct relationship a grandchild has to the Sales Process Map. If you were not asking, you're asking now—the direct relationship is that through the use of the map, more options came into my life. I actually became more valuable than I already was, earned a higher income (W-2), and while I was at it, carved out more leisure time to hang out with my granddaughter.

Here's a risk taking paragraph for you: In a previous section of this work, I mentioned uniting lifetime learning, musicianship and meditation. Lifetime learning should be quite evident by now. Musicianship is presented below. What of meditation? Can meditation and Sales Process Mapping be used in the same sentence? That was easy. My meditation practice began on January 20, 1973, the second inauguration of a troubled U.S. President. That's nearly forty years of almost daily meditation—I take one day off each week. And yes, I can still sit on the floor despite my advancing age. I would have to say that this practice has been enormously beneficial, but there is no way of accurately assessing this statement. Where would I be today without having experienced a virtual lifetime of meditation? I'll meditate on that. Incidentally, the most difficult part of meditation is putting it on your calendar.

...And oh, yes, an inner passion of music. I wrote down a goal of recording with So-and-So at a time when I didn't know if I might have to pawn my equipment, after having been a highly regarded registered honcho in the insurance majors. I still haven't recorded with So-and-So. But the resources that have materialized from my business have put me in a position where I was able to produce a second CD in collaboration with musicians of a caliber that could only have been dreamed of over fifteen years ago.

OK, before you ask—go to www.Hellboys.com. Yes, that's the name of the band—it's a good thing that I don't need a real job.

And now, ladies and gentlemen, it is a privilege to introduce these very generous and incredibly skilled musicians of The Hell-boys:

Tony Levin is an American rock musician, specializing in bass guitar and Chapman Stick.

Robert Fripp is an English guitarist, composer and record producer.

Tom Redmond is an American guitarist, composer, singer and record producer.

Carolyn Redmond, one of the daughters of Tom Redmond, is a percussionist and managed the production and fulfillment of the CD's. Carolyn collects the money.

Vora Vor is an American guitarist, composer, singer and record producer.

Curt Golden is an American guitarist, composer, singer and record producer.

Bill Rieflin is an American musician, most active as a drummer.

Jerry Marotta is a much-sought-after studio and live performance drummer.

The California Guitar Trio is made up of Bert Lams, Hideyo Moriya and Paul Richards. Just go check them out: www.CGTrio.com.

Bill Forth is an American guitarist, composer, singer and record producer.

Kelli Rae Powell is an incredible vocalist.

Victor McSurely is an American guitarist, composer, singer and off-Broadway house musician specializing in the Stick.

Luciano Pietrafesa is an Argentinean guitarist—just go to www.Zumguitars.com.

Tony Geballe is an American guitarist, composer and absurdly wondrous record producer.

These players enjoy working with The Hellboys since there are no meetings to attend.

Selling from the Inside Out: The Map to Spectacular Sales Success in Business and in Life was the differentiating factor. What else could it have been? The map flies in the window, I write it down, take a leap from a high-paying career, follow the map, and am now regularly recording with some of the best musicians on the planet. Not to mention writing a book about how to apply these same principles, techniques and thinking to *your* life. Here's a way to make you more valuable than you already are. Here's a way to have more options in your life.

…and a Sense of Humor is Helpful…

And thank you, Joanne, for being the love of my life. And Sarah and Hannah and Carolyn—all loves of my life. What rare blessings.

About the Author

Thomas M. Redmond, Jr. is the founder and president of Redmond Group, Inc. Launched late in the last century (1996), the firm specializes in evaluating and improving client sales processes. Tom has over forty years of experience, with specific expertise in the generation and management of sales. For the last fifteen+ years, his firm has successfully assisted clients in designing systematic sales processes, process maps, and measurement protocols for new business development. He has worked with thousands of sales professionals conducting in-person workshops, seminars, webcasts and public speaking appearances. His practice also includes one-on-one coaching with individual sales professionals, sales managers, and sales teams supplemented by a monthly Sales Coach Newsletter with over 4,500 subscribers. His clients include multi-billion dollar companies like Chubb & Son, Fireman's Fund, Great American, Zurich, Liberty Mutual, Safeco, Mass Mutual, CNA, Marsh, Willis, A.J Gallagher, and many independent insurance agents and brokers.

Prior to starting his own firm, Tom's employment included positions with global insurance brokers, primarily in the commercial property and casualty insurance segment. During his tenure with these brokers, he led and managed a variety of specialty insurance product teams, the largest personal lines facility in the country, several profit centers, and the North American aviation and aerospace division. He also acted as broker and account manager on complex multi-national clients.

Tom's pedigree is soaked in the insurance business: grandfather, father, mother, uncles, brothers, and perhaps most surprisingly, his DNA has been linked to that of "Risky," the remains of a 1.2 million-year-old hominid recently discovered in Tanzania amid artifacts that include what appears to be a primitive actuarial table and leading indicator metrics.

His educational background includes a B.S. in industrial relations and management from Seton Hall University, the prestigious Chartered Property and Casualty Underwriter (CPCU) designation, and he is a certified instructor on Overcoming Call Reluctance. Tom is a frequent speaker and writer on the subjects of sales strategies, techniques, and client service. We invite the readers to visit www.Redmondgroupinc.com for further information and a glimpse of the monthly newsletters that offer solid follow-up to sales professionals. Don't overlook Tom's "Sales Excuse of the Day" and the remedies that are available.

Due to his background as a "street-level," frontline sales executive, Tom delivers a unique perspective and empathy with today's and tomorrow's salesperson. From entry-level salespeople to high-performing producers and senior management, Tom has the ability to win over his audience and create a strong sense of loyalty, enthusiasm, and commitment to action. He's also funny.

Tom lives in Middletown, New Jersey with his wife, a few koi, and there is a Cavalier King Charles spaniel in their future. World headquarters for Redmond Group is in Middletown, New Jersey. Come visit www.Redmondgroupinc.com, or better yet, call us at 732-957-0005.

For downloadable versions of other Sales Process Maps, the Excel Tracking Masters and Transition Chart, please refer to our website, www.Redmondgroupinc.com.

CPSIA information can be obtained
at www.ICGtesting.com
Printed in the USA
FFHW021036040519
52243216-57633FF